GROW
YOUR
OWN
DWARF
FRUIT
TREES

GROW YOUR OWN DWARF FRUIT TREES

Ken and Pat Kraft

Illustrated by Thuy Le Ha

WALKER AND COMPANY

NEW YORK

This book is for
Barbara Lowenstein,
friend, adviser,
and editor par excellence.

For help of various sorts during the course of writing this book, we are grateful to the many who have responded to our need for guidance, advice, materials, and other assistance. Among them are Howard Boksenbaum at the Center for the Biology of Natural Systems, Miss Beatrice F. Hewitt, Robert A. Nitschke, Don L. Rogers, Lloyd S. Stark, and Paul Stark, Jr.' In addition we are, as always, most appreciative of the expert help given us by the staff of the Harrison Mevorial Library of Carmel, California, and of the particular efforts of Mrs. Vicki Jones and Mrs. Sheila Baldridge.

First photo in chapter 1 and photos in chapters 3, 6 and 8—Stark Bro's Nurseries
Second and third photos in chapter 1—USDA and photos in chapter 4 and 9 —USDA
Fourth photo in chapter 1 and photo in chapter 5—Armstrong Nurseries

First published in the United States of America in 1974 by the Walker Publishing Company, Inc.

Published simultaneously in Canada by Fitzhenry & Whiteside, Limited, Toronto

Library of Congress Catalog Card Number: 73-83296

ISBN: 0-8027-0429-8

Printed in the United States of America.

10 9 8 7 6 5 4 3 2 1

CONTENTS

1

Dwarfs for Fruits, Fun, and Flexibility

There are about 85 million home gardeners in the United States, according to a recent estimate, and every day more of them start wondering about the same thing that two friends of ours, Bill and Joyce, asked us the other day: "Is there any hope that we could grow enough fruit here in our little yard to make the effort really worthwhile?" Bill said. "Like apples?"

He was talking about a dab of ground at one end of their back garden, a spot perhaps 10 feet wide by 20 feet long where a few shrubs were growing. The piece of ground wasn't even one quarter enough to accommodate a regular-sized apple tree—the size called "standard" by nurserymen. However, we weren't thinking of a standard apple tree just then. In the 10-by-20-foot spot, two *dwarf* apple trees could fit without crowding each other, and as many as six could fit if they were planted toward the outer edges of the 20-foot sides.

So . . . "Would a couple of hundred pounds of apples be 'worthwhile'?" one of us asked. Apples were just then selling at about forty cents a pound at the supermarket.

"You mean *every year?*" Joyce exclaimed after a startled moment. *"Two hundred pounds* of apples?"

We said it was a reasonable production for two mature dwarf apple trees. It amounts to about two bushels per tree. Even three bushels per year from a dwarf apple tree isn't an uncommon yield, and the very thrifty spur-type dwarf apple trees—the kind that have fruit-bearing wood, called spurs, clustered thickly on the branches and even on the trunk—can astonish a home gardener with as much as six bushels. That's 300 pounds of apples in a single dazzling harvest. Two such full grown trees on that 10-by-20-foot bit of ground might grow their lucky owners over a *quarter ton* of fresh, juicy, healthful apples in one season.

Most people don't realize this. When they think of a dwarf fruit tree, what comes to mind is a pretty little thing on the lawn that might even become a conversation piece by bearing a few fruits.

This idea wasn't so far off the track a few years ago. Today it's outdated and wrong. There has been a great deal of good work done to develop dwarf fruit trees that really work for a living. This is especially so with apples —so much that even commercial growers are now planting acres of dwarf apple trees; nobody needs further proof that today's dwarf trees are a far, far different breed of fruit producer than those of years ago.

In addition to dwarf apple trees, you can get good little dwarf trees in pears, peaches, nectarines, plums, cherries, and apricots. We'll talk about all of these in the chapters that follow.

WHAT IS A DWARF?

A dwarf fruit tree is a small tree that bears regular-sized fruit. There are various sizes of dwarf trees, from little ones about as small as rose bushes, to some about two thirds the size of standard-sized fruit trees. Each

The fruits borne by a dwarf tree are as large as those on the same variety of a standard-sized tree, as shown by the big Starkrimson apples this little girl is picking from a tree not twice as tall as she is.

kind has advantages for certain uses and locations, but the types we'll be talking about for the most part will be the little dwarfs, from rose bush size on up to those not much taller than a good-sized man.

WHAT MAKES A DWARF A DWARF?

You might well wonder how a dwarf tree gets that way. In general, it does so in one of two ways. It is either a dwarf by nature (genetic dwarf), or is dwarfed by man —usually by grafting a standard fruit-bearing top onto a root system (rootstock) of a natural dwarf. If a tree's roots are those of a dwarf, the entire tree will be dwarfed. Experiments have also shown that if *any* part of a grafted tree is from a genetic dwarf, it will more or less dwarf the tree; but the use of a dwarfing rootstock is the most usual method.

Rootstocks themselves, by the way, are multiplied by rooting cuttings the same way home gardeners start a new plant by rooting a stem (slip) of a mature plant in moist soil. For fruit-tree rootstocks, the stem is cut in late fall, rooted during the winter, and then transplanted outdoors. It will be ready to receive a graft toward the end of the growing season.

Most of the dwarf trees we will be talking about are grafted dwarfs. The roots are those of natural (genetic) dwarfs, and fruit-bearing tops from standard-sized trees have been grafted on to these dwarfed rootstocks. Since the roots are here the whole reason for the dwarfing, let's take a minute to see what these dwarfing rootstocks are, because there is quite a choice of them.

Apples

The work done at the East Malling Research Station in Kent, England, is responsible for standardizing the rootstocks now most widely used for dwarfing apple trees. This work, dating from the World War I period, sorted out all the well-known genetic dwarf rootstocks and classified the best of them according to their dwarfing effects. This classification system uses the initials EM (to stand for East Malling), or just M, followed by a Roman numeral, though now Americans more often use the more familiar Arabic numerals. Thus, the designation EM 9

This is what a stempiece apple tree looks like in the nursery row. The dwarfing stempiece is labeled B. Below it, labeled A, is the rootstock. Above the stempiece is the scion, labeled C, and in this case Golden Delicious, which will become the entire fruit-bearing part of the tree.

Just ten years old and bearing regular crops for several years, this dwarf McIntosh apple in blossom is only about 8' tall. A normal annual harvest is upward of a hundred pounds of apples from a dwarf tree as mature and well-grown as this one.

refers to the rootstock that usually makes the smallest dwarf apple tree, about 6 to 8 feet tall. There is now a still more dwarfing rootstock, EM 27, but it is still under test and not yet available, so we mention it only as a matter of future interest in the garden.

Other East Malling rootstocks—among them EM 1, EM 2, EM 4, and EM 7—produce small apple trees, though usually not as small as EM 9 does. But because fruit trees, like people, don't always behave the way you expect them to, certain varieties of apples will be less dwarfed by a particular dwarfing rootstock than other varieties grafted to the same rootstock. Additional factors, such as disease resistance and strengths of graft unions must be taken into account by horticulturists.

One way around some problems has been to use a piece of wood from a dwarf as part of the *trunk* of a young apple tree, instead of using dwarf-tree roots. This dwarfing trunk section is called a *stempiece* or *interstock*, and although the method is more than 300 years old, it was not often used, so seemed almost new when it came to notice again in the 1930s under the name of the Clark Dwarf.

To someone unfamiliar with the mysteries of grafting, a Clark Dwarf tree is a miracle. Its roots are those of a sturdy apple tree such as a crabapple; the lower part of its trunk is from a very strong-trunked variety of apple tree; the upper part of the trunk is from a third tree, a very winter-hardy natural dwarf apple; and the fruit-bearing top is from still a *fourth* variety. This version of a stempiece-grafted tree was called a Clark Dwarf after the man, an amateur fruit gardener who discovered the original winter-hardy natural dwarf apple tree (he found it growing in a home garden in Iowa). This discovery interested horticulturists at Iowa State University because Iowa winters were so hard on other dwarf apple trees that they were killed, and the horticulturists were searching for something better. The Clark Dwarf certainly was better—so much so that it soon was introduced to the trade by the big Missouri-based Stark Bro's Nurseries, which was well accustomed to the rigors of Midwest winters. They have been using the procedure, or variations of it ever since.

The way a nursery grows such a stempiece tree is to graft a piece of living wood from a strong-trunked variety onto a strong-rooted young seedling tree. (In nurserymen's language: "Graft a hardy trunk on apple seedling root.") After this two-piece tree grows for a season, a two-piece graft consisting of a length of Clark Dwarf below and the fruit-bearing variety above is grafted to the little tree, whereupon the whole thing grows into the final four-piece mature tree.

A stempiece, by the way, is just a few inches long, but a curious point here is that its length determines to a good degree how tall the dwarf tree will grow. Experiments at Cornell University in 1966 showed that McIntosh dwarfs with two-inch stempieces grew nearly eleven feet tall, while those with seven-inch stempieces were much shorter—under seven feet. In case you are led to assume from this that the longer the stempiece, the shorter the tree, don't. An eight-inch stempiece grew a taller tree than the seven-inch one.

Pears

After the complexities and variations of apple-dwarfing, that of pears seems happily simple. To dwarf a pear tree, a variety of the kind wanted to produce fruit is simply grafted onto the rootstock of a quince. The quinces employed for this are usually Angers and Provence, which are more *types* than varieties. Although this pear-quince combination may seem an odd marriage (the two are distantly related, however), it succeeds beautifully in most cases. Where it won't succeed, due to the unwillingness of some varieties of pear to grow on quince roots—appropriately called incompatibility—the solution is to graft a stempiece of a compatible variety onto the quince roots, and then graft to this stempiece the variety that will bear the fruit. The compatible pear that is generally used for this purpose has the agreeable name of Old Home. Another very good one for this bridging purpose is a pear called Beurre Hardy.

Peaches

The best dwarf trees we have in peaches are genetic dwarfs with lovely blossoms and dense foliage, pretty little things that will grow nicely in a tub and are a pleasure to have around for their looks alone. They start bearing early, and usually get no taller than six feet. Their ancestor is Swatow, a natural dwarf peach from China. Credit for developing from this bloodline the first truly edible genetic dwarf, named Bonanza, goes to the Armstrong Nurseries.

Dwarf peaches are also propagated by grafting scions of standard-sized peach trees onto dwarfing rootstocks, although the results are less satisfactory than with apples. The dwarfing rootstocks for peach are most often two species of cherry, the Western Sand cherry and the Nanking cherry, and a plum called St. Julien A, which is related to Damson plums. The Western Sand cherry is a shrub up to five feet tall; it grows wild on the prairies of North America. The Nanking cherry is native to Central Asia and is a bush-like plant. The St. Julien A, like its Damson relatives, is by nature a dwarfish and compact tree.

Nectarines

A nectarine can be described as a fuzzless peach. It is sometimes dwarfed by being grafted onto the same dwarfing rootstocks that serve for dwarfing the peach tree. Also, like the peach, there are newly developed genetic dwarfs (which may be grown on standard rootstocks without losing their dwarf character), and what we have just said of the genetic dwarf peaches goes with equal force for the nectarines. Armstrong Nurseries were also the breeders of one of the first successful yellow-fleshed nectarines of this class, Nectarina.

This thrifty little genetic dwarf peach tree, the Bonanza variety, can be considered an ornamental that bears good fruit. Notice the close-spaced and attractive foliage, and the fine size of the fruits. Now not even as tall as the child beside it, the tree will get no taller than about 6', even when fully grown.

Plums

Plums, as with peaches, are grown fairly successfully in dwarf-tree size by grafting scions of them onto rootstocks of Western Sand cherry and the Nanking cherry.

Cherries

The newest and best development in dwarf cherry trees came a few years ago from the Minnesota Fruit Breeding Farm. It is a hybrid, a tart cherry called North Star that grows about eight feet tall. It also is being used as a rootstock for dwarfing some sweet cherries. The ground cherry, a four-foot bush form from Siberia, has also been used as a dwarfing rootstock, but not with notable success so far. The well-known tart cherry Montmorency is also used as a somewhat dwarfing rootstock in this way, since tart cherries are naturally smaller trees than most sweet cherries.

In this same way, rootstocks of a wild sweet cherry, the mazzard, and rootstocks of the perfume cherry of Europe, the mahaleb, are commonly used and have a somewhat dwarfing effect—but only somewhat, and we can't call the resulting trees really dwarfed. Nor can we say it of Meteor, a tart semi-dwarf that grows up to 15 feet tall. All in all, North Star is the best dwarf cherry available at this time, even though it grows a bit taller than the height of an average man. We should add, however, that when a cherry tree is much smaller than this, its crop is not large enough to satisfy many gardeners. So the really dwarfed cherry tree is gradually being dropped by nurseries.

Apricots

Like peaches and plums, apricots are dwarfed by grafting them onto Western Sand cherry and Nanking cherry rootstocks. Many other rootstocks have been tested but none has yet come into wide use.

WHY PLANT DWARFS?

If you have only a little space, like our friends Bill and Joyce, a dwarf fruit tree is in most cases the only fruit tree that will fit and thrive there. But suppose you have plenty of space, say a piece of open ground measuring 80 feet by 80 feet. You could plant two standard apple trees, two standard peach trees, two standard nectarine trees, a couple of sour cherry trees, and two Japanese plum trees —just to pick a selection at random. It is a good selection, though, and will give a family much more fruit than they'd ever dream of buying at the market. They would have ten trees in their little orchard. So . . . with all that space why would anyone plant dwarf trees instead? For several reasons. Here are the more important.

AN 80' x 80' PLOT PLANTED TO STANDARD FRUIT TREES

80'

1 apple		1 apple	
1 peach	1 peach	1 nectarine	1 nectarine
1 sour cherry	1 Japanese plum	1 Japanese plum	1 sour cherry

80'

N ↑

1" - 20'

• On that same piece of ground you could plant about 60 dwarf fruit trees and get a far wider selection of kinds and varieties; 16 varieties of apples, for instance, instead of only two;

AN 80' x 80' PLOT PLANTED TO DWARF FRUIT TREES

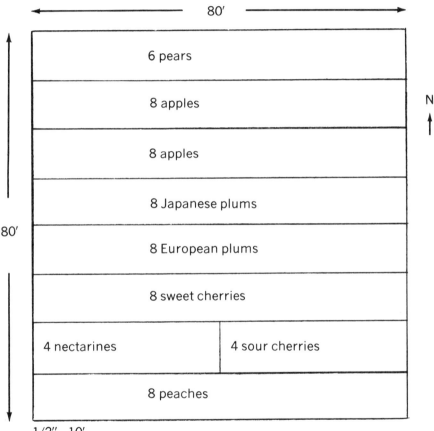

80'

6 pears

8 apples

8 apples

8 Japanese plums

8 European plums

8 sweet cherries

4 nectarines | 4 sour cherries

8 peaches

N

1/2" - 10'

eight varieties of peaches instead of two; eight varieties of peaches instead of two; eight Japanese plums instead of two; four sour cherries instead of two; and four nectarines instead of two. In addition, you'd get some kinds of fruits you wouldn't even have space for in the other planting—six pear trees, eight sweet cherry trees, and eight European plum trees.

•   In addition to being more fun, this far greater spread of varieties and kinds of fruits from the dwarfs also provides a margin of safety in case a variety doesn't do as well as expected one year; with a standard-sized tree this might wipe out the whole crop, but with the several varieties of dwarfs you can still count on a good harvest from unaffected trees.

•   Dwarfs have a fine reputation for giving a quick return on an investment. Instead of keeping you waiting three to five years for a crop from a standard-sized tree, a dwarf tree usually starts bearing the year you plant it, or the year after. The New York State Fruit Testing Cooperative Association (see Chapter 10) recognizes this dwarf characteristic by grafting new varieties of apples and pears on dwarfing rootstocks for the purpose of inducing early bearing and thus getting a faster evaluation.

•   Dwarf trees have been rated as more efficient than large trees, using more of their nutrients to make fruit instead of wood.

•   The fruit from a dwarf tree is the same size and the same in all other respects as that from a standard-sized tree of the same variety. If anything, the fruit from the dwarf will be a little bigger.

•   A dwarf tree is a handy size to care for. To prune and harvest a standard-sized tree you need a ladder and other such equipment for extending your reach, but with a dwarf you don't even need a step-stool most of the time.

• This compact size of the dwarf also makes it as easy to spray as a rose bush. And you use far less spray or dust than on a big tree—about a quart of spray compared to 30 or 40 quarts for the standard-sized tree.

• And although any fruit tree is a beautiful part of a home planting, here the dwarfs are outstanding—lovely bouquets at eye-level, followed by flashing colors and softly rounded forms of the ripening fruit—ornaments you can eat.

• For growing up a wall or framework as an espalier, the dwarf tree is *the* tree, a docile little fellow that takes to training. (See Chapter 6.) And if you want a tree you can move around, to enjoy in different locations from time to time, or to protect from severe weather by moving it under shelter, a dwarf is willing to live in a tub. (See Chapter 5.)

• If by now you are sold on dwarfs except for one niggling little doubt—"But aren't they awfully short-lived?"—don't give it another thought. Dwarfs have close to the same life expectancy as their standard-sized relatives. Perhaps the notion they die young took hold because the average standard fruit tree will live through neglect that could discourage a dwarf with its shallower root system. Give your dwarf trees decent care and your grandchildren can be picking fruit in the twenty-first century from the dwarf apple and pear trees you are planting now.

WHAT ABOUT THE 5-ON-1 DWARF?

You've probably seen ads offering dwarf trees that bear three to five different fruits—such as two peaches, two plums, and cherries—or ones that bear three to five different varieties of the same fruit on the same tree, such as varieties of apples. The first kind is a risky buy, so much so that the National Better Business Bureau has cautioned home gardeners against expecting much from such trees. The reason for this caution is the frequency of failure for grafts of *different species* on the same rootstock. It's "agin nature," you could say. The dwarf tree with several varieties of the *same species* grafted on it, however—be they all apples, pears, peaches, or whatever —is more likely to succeed. And even though this kind of tree too is a 9-day wonder to behold, fruit breeders have used this system to speed up testing of new varieties. Luther Burbank, the first plant breeder to call wide attention to the technique, if not the first to use it, carried it to such lengths that he was said to have grafted 1000 different new apple varieties on a single apple tree in his yard.

WHAT ARE THE RIGHT DWARFS FOR YOU?

To calculate your chances of success with the mini-orchard you are planning, answer these two questions as honestly as you can.

> 1.   What fruits do you like most of all? If you adore peaches, then peaches, not plums or pears, are the thing for you to grow for yourself. If this seems so obvious as not to need mentioning, you'd be surprised at how many home gardeners are growing some fruit for a reason other than a great liking for it. One depressingly common such reason is that another gardener offered them a free tree. Another is that they happened to pass a nursery sale display and got carried away with the idea of growing fruit, any fruit.

2. What *can* you grow? Here again, this basic point is often blithely ignored. We'll take up various necessities of dwarf fruit trees in the chapters that follow, but for quick reference, here are the things to keep in mind when populating your dwarf orchard:

Space

Figure on a 10-by-10-foot space for each tree; pears will be happier with 12-by-12-feet, though they'll get along with less. You *can* crowd dwarfs, but we recommend not doing it because crowding is a contributing factor in some diseases.

Climate

If you live where winters are so mild that you never need anti-freeze in the car, trees such as apple and peach that need winter chilling may not bear fruit for you. And if you live in a rugged winter climate, no sweet cherry (except the bush cherries—see Chapter 8) will do well, nor will non-hardy varieties of peaches, apples, and other fruits. If your climate has late spring frosts, forget apricots. For more details on all this, see the individual species in Chapter 4.

Time

Here we mean your own time. Dwarf fruit trees take far less gardening time than most flowers and vegetables planted on the same amount of ground, but any plant needs some attention. Figure on giving a dwarf tree one hour of pruning per season, two to five hours of pest control, an hour of harvesting, and about three hours of miscellaneous care. That's between seven and ten hours a season; fair enough?

Site

A dwarf tree, to do well, needs an open spot, on fertile soil, well drained, without big trees and their greedy roots nearby. It will need some watering in long dry spells, so the site should be near a water line. And if you have such predators as deer in the area, the site requires a fence around it.

2

The First Year

In this chapter we're going to tell how to get your own dwarf-fruit mini-orchard started. We will take up these first-year points in this order: How to choose and prepare the place where your dwarf fruit trees are to grow; how to get the trees, and get the right ones for you; how to plant the trees for a successful bearing life; how to give a dwarf tree its first pruning; how to set up a compost-making project that will provide you with a constant and steady supply of a natural fertilizing mulch.

WHERE TO PLANT YOUR DWARF TREES

Even before you decide where to get your trees and what fruits to get, you positively must settle on where you'll plant them. The reason is that fruit trees are for the long pull. Even a peach, which is considered short-lived, will be with you for the next ten years or more. Therefore you want to be sure to pick a place that you, and hopefully the peach, will still be satisfied with ten years from now—and make that a good thirty, forty,

A dwarf orchard can be planted on a sunny patch of the house grounds, as are these half-dozen little apple, pear, and peach trees in a Missouri gardener's back yard, and can return a yearly harvest of several hundred pounds of fruit.

fifty, and more years for some of the other fruits.

A dwarf tree never gets immense, so you needn't worry about it eventually growing up and smothering the house if you plant it nearby; nor will it grow so tall it may bomb you with ripe fruit in season. Dwarf fruit trees are in fact nice to have near the house; they also serve as landscape groupings on the house grounds, as accent plantings at one end of a walk, as a grove on both sides of a walk or driveway, or as a screening planting near a lot boundary or around a summerhouse. But remember—in any such locations as these you will be taking a certain amount of chance. This is because you'll be putting your own interests first in choosing the place for the trees, and the place you choose may not be so very popular with the trees. We merely mention this, though. Personally, we take the view that dwarf fruit trees (or anything else we plant) were made for us, not we for them, and so we please ourselves first, within reason, and sometimes lose, but we accept this risk.

If you're lucky, though, the spot you choose will have: fertile soil that is a pleasure to work with, and that drains well enough so that it never becomes swampy but doesn't go bone dry ten minutes after the rain stops; a gently sloping site, because cooler air rolls down a slope, ventilating the little trees, which helps keep them healthy; sunshine for most of the day, because this is a health factor, a growth factor, and helps to ripen fruit; protection from hard winds; convenience to water, tools, and any future deliveries of mulching materials or other bulky supplies; proximity to the house so you can keep an eye on the trees at certain times—harvest time, for instance, when birds have plans to get there before you do; no nearby big trees or heavy shrubbery plantings to compete with the dwarf fruit trees for nourishment and moisture.

PREPARING THE PLANTING SITE

We have known some gardeners fortunate enough to have an extra piece of ground alongside their house lot on which to plant dwarf trees. Should you have such a fairly open piece of ground, we suggest you start your preparations for the dwarf trees several months ahead of time by planting the land with a legume such as crimson clover, alfalfa, or whatever does well in your area. Your county agent can advise you here. Do this planting in early summer, and turn the crop under in the fall. A rotary tiller is a good tool for doing this, and one can be rented. A crop of this sort is called a cover crop, and when you turn it under, you are "green-manuring," in farm terms. The object is to add a lot of organic matter to the soil, which helps it hold more water and also adds nutrients. A pound of seed will sow about 1000 square feet of land, such as a plot 20 by 50 feet. The only exception to this procedure is land that is already terribly rich in organic matter, and there is very little of that. See Chapter 10 for locating your county agent and other government sources of information.

An alternative to green-manuring is to cover the ground with something such as straw or leaves or chopped weeds, and let this cover lie there during the fall and winter. This is called a mulch, and it usually isn't turned under the way the cover crop is, but stays on top of the ground and conserves moisture; when planting the dwarf trees in the spring, the mulch is merely pulled away enough so the holes can be dug, and is then raked back around the trees. We have found that a mulch of this kind is a good way to tame difficult clay soil.

A third method of preparing the planting site ahead of time is actually a combination of the others. Dig the holes for the trees the previous fall, and then fill these holes with straw, leaves, etc. as soon as they are dug; manure or a slow fertilizer can be added. By spring planting time the material in the holes has pretty well broken down into compost, and it is mixed with the earth dug out of the holes, then used to refill the holes when the trees are planted.

One other item we ought to bring up at this early stage is the matter of a soil test to determine pH value, an acidity measurement. Fruit trees will grow in any soil a vegetable garden will grow in, that is, a soil which ranges anywhere from slightly acid to just slightly alkaline. A slightly acid soil, from 5.5 to 6.5 on the pH scale, is best. If you'd feel better knowing the degree of acidity, get a soil test, or make one. See Chapter 10 for addresses. To make soil less acid, you broadcast lime, such as the easily found hydrated lime. Fall is the best time to do this, and the amount varies from one to five pounds per 100 square feet, depending on how much correction is needed. To make soil *more* acid (not usually needed except in certain alkaline regions) you can work rotted sawdust or peat moss into the planting spots, a bushel or two per spot for dwarf trees.

HOW TO GET YOUR DWARF TREES

The trees you will be planting will be one or two years old in most cases, grown by a nursery. The nurseryman will have accomplished the job by sprouting a tree from a seed or by rooting a cutting, usually, then grafting a scion to this stripling. The scion is from a variety of fruit tree that will grow on the other and will become the top of the new tree, producing the fruit. To make this two-part tree (or three-part, or four-part, as noted in Chapter 1) is a good deal of work by hand, and you know what hand work costs today, so it isn't surprising that dwarf trees usually aren't low in cost. One mail-order nursery, for example, that charges $4 for a standard-sized apple tree, charges $6.90 for a dwarf apple. Another nursery has a still wider spread—$3.45 for a standard and $9.25 for a dwarf. But a more common differential is two or three dollars, and the average price today for a dwarf fruit tree is between $5 and $6. Most nurseries add a packing charge to the order (50 cents is typical), and most of them add the cost of shipping, usually done by Parcel Post. Some nurseries, though, more or less offset these charges by including a free tree with the order.

If you deal with a local nursery you'll probably save some of these costs. But so much nursery stock is sold by mail-order nurseries, and such a wide choice of varieties is thereby available to the home gardener, we assume most readers of this book will want to know what the mail-order nurseries offer them. You will find a list of most of the big ones, along with several smaller ones and some good specialty nurseries, in Chapter 10. And to make the references to varieties more useful, particularly in Chapters 4, 7, and 8, we follow the description of each variety with the names of the nurseries that sell it. Consequently, we have made it a rule to find out if a variety is easily available before describing it, as there seems no point in talking at length about some wonder that you haven't a prayer of getting. To obtain a nursery catalog, just send a postcard request to any of the nurseries we list, making sure you write your name and address on the postcard. The only nurseries on the list currently making a charge for catalogs are Leuthardt, 25 cents; New York State Fruit Testing Cooperative Association, a $4 membership fee; and Southmeadow, $1 for its complete catalog but no charge for its price list. Most catalogs are issued very early in the year or even before, and supplies of the catalogs may run out in early spring, so try to get your requests mailed no later than February.

By the time you get your catalog, or catalogs, we'll assume you will have a working idea of what fruits you want to plant, taking a cue from your own tastes and from the descriptions of varieties in this book and any others you have consulted. So, when you look over the catalogs, pay particular attention to two points about any variety you are interested in:

1. Its adaptability to your climate
2. Its pollination requirements.

Climate Adaptability

The Plant Hardiness Zone Map in Chapter 4 will give you a quick reference to your area's *general* winter climate. For example, if you live in Zone 6, you can expect the coldest winter temperatures to range from about 0° F. to -10° F. This is strictly an average, and as we can testify to from experience, parts of Zone 6 have had winters when the thermometer sank to nearer -20° F. than -10° F. However, the zonal map will be a help in deciding what you can reasonably expect to grow.

Keep these points in mind when looking at the map: If you live near the boundary line of a zone, your average winter temperatures will be close to those of the adjoining zone; there are also varying climates within a zone, not always indicated on the map, but colder or milder than the zone average because they are in high elevations (colder), or near large bodies of water (milder).

Remember too that temperatures are only one factor in plant growth. Some others are the length of the growing season, rainfall, day length, sunlight intensity, humidity, summer heat, force of wind, soil characteristics, and air purity. Some of these things you can alter if necessary, but you can't do much about the length of the growing season, day length, humidity, and winter temperatures.

It is helpful to know that all the trees we are talking about in this book *need* some cold weather in winter. If they don't get it, the dormant state they slip into after the growing season is over—a kind of hibernation—just continues; it takes some cold weather to wake them up and get ready for spring, and if they don't get it, their spring growth is slow and haphazard, and they aren't worth fooling with. This is usually the case when someone living in a mild climate such as southern California or the Gulf Coast insists on planting an apple tree he grew in Michigan, since all but a few apples need winter cold. The term for this is "chilling requirement."

Extreme winter cold, however, can kill flower buds and there won't be any fruit that season. Of the trees we cover here, peaches, nectarines, and sweet cherries are the most vulnerable. Buds of most varieties of peaches and nectarines may be killed if midwinter temperatures drop to -10° F., and sweet cherry trees can be hurt if winter cold comes so early that the trees are not yet dormant.

As a general guide, here are the various fruits and

their zonal ranges (see the complete zone map in Chapter 4):

Apples. Zones 4 to 8. A few very hardy kinds will grow in Zone 3 and even in Zone 2. A few with low winter chilling requirements will fruit in Zones 9 and 10. Best known of these is Winter Banana (see Chapter 8 under Fruit Varieties for Problem Areas); others may be had from local nurseries.

Pears. Zones 5 to 8 for most pears. Kieffer and a few other hardy ones will grow in Zone 4; Kieffer also grows in Zone 9.

Peaches and Nectarines. Zones 5 to 8 for most varieties, with a few hardy ones thriving in Zone 4, and a few accepting the mild winters of Zone 9.

Japanese plums. Usually do well where most peaches grow, Zones 5 to 9.

European plums. Usually do well where most pears grow, Zones 5 to 7.

Damson plums. Winter-hardy, they do best in Zones 5 to 7.

Sour cherries. Zones 4 to 7, though a few varieties will fruit in cooler parts of Zone 8.

Sweet cherries. Zones 5 to 7, with a few varieties accepting the winter cold of Zone 4.

Apricots. Like peaches, most grow in Zones 5 to 8.

Pollination Requirements

As regards pollination, many fruit trees won't grow

fruit unless their blossoms are pollinated by pollen from a different variety of the same fruit. The general rules are:

Apples, Pears, Plums, Sweet cherries. Nearly all varieties need a different variety planted nearby, so are said to be "self-unfruitful" or "self-sterile."

Peaches, Nectarines, Sour cherries, Apricots. Most will set fruit without a different variety nearby, so are said to be "self-fruitful."

At this point you may be remembering a fruit tree that was growing all by itself somewhere and bearing regular crops of fruit, even though it was in one of those groups we named above as self-sterile. So what about that? It is a fairly common experience, and the answer is: It was receiving pollen, via bees, from some other compatible variety growing in the neighborhood. The other variety could even be growing a few blocks away if the busy bees were busy enough. But depending on somebody else to grow the right tree for your purpose is chancy. We'll go into pollination requirements further in Chapter 4.

PLANTING THE TREES

Spring planting, as early as possible, is the rule for most fruit trees. In mild climates they can also be planted in late fall, but except for cherries, fall planting can be considered second-best. If a nursery offers you a choice of ages in trees, choose the youngest; even though it will probably be smaller, the younger the tree, the better it will transplant.

If you buy from a mail-order nursery, your trees will arrive well-wrapped so the roots, which will be bare, stay moist. But don't take chances. Unwrap the package promptly, and if the roots feel dry, stand the young trees with their roots in a tub of water. Prune off any broken roots at this time. In some states, such as California, inspectors open nursery packages from out-of-state, so it behooves gardeners there to hustle for their nursery stock as soon as the Post Office tells them it can be picked up.

The trees can stand in the tub of water for 24 hours if you can plant them soon after. If you or the weather aren't ready for planting by then, a good old-fashioned

HEELING IN NURSERY STOCK

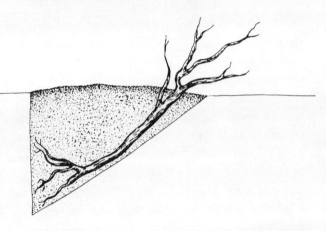

way to keep the trees happy is to heel them into the earth. Pick a shady spot, as on the north side of a building, dig a wedge-shaped trench as illustrated, lay the young trees on the slanting side of the trench, and cover the roots with the earth you dug out. Protected in this way, the trees will be all right until you plant them.

The next step in planting is to dig a good big hole for each tree. Space these holes 10 feet apart, center to center, or a little more if you have the room. Dig them at least 2 feet deep, and wide enough so you can spread the tree's roots with room to spare. The trees may not be planted 2 feet deep, as we'll see presently, but by digging that deep, you will help future drainage. As you dig, lay the topsoil to one side so that when you refill the hole you

PLANTING A TREE WITH A DWARFING ROOTSTOCK

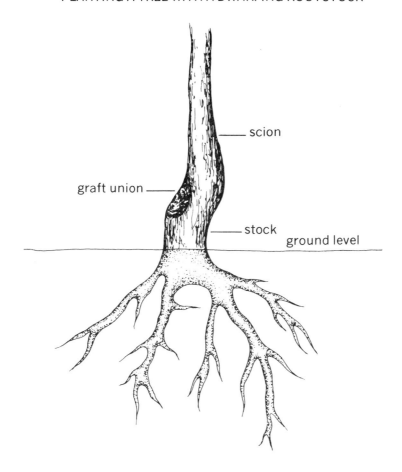

can put the topsoil at the bottom; it is the most fertile soil, so you want it in contact with the roots. We also like to mix some compost with this soil, about a bushel per tree. This provides a mild fertilizing and helps the soil structure.

While you are digging the holes, protect the roots of the trees from sun and air by keeping a damp burlap sack over them.

Now you are ready to set the trees in the holes. To tell how deeply to set a tree, lay a narrow board across the hole to show where the ground level will be when the hole is refilled. Then set the tree in the hole, and hold its trunk against the edge of the board at a height that places the graft union (a kink in the trunk) a few inches *above* ground level, as illustrated. This is also the depth at which the tree had been growing in the nursery, as you can tell by the lighter color of the trunk part that was above ground. The reason for keeping the graft union above ground level is that if it gets buried, the top part of

PLANTING A TREE WITH A DWARFING STEMPIECE

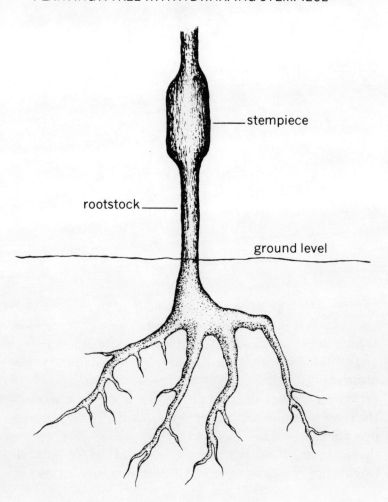

stempiece

rootstock

ground level

STAKING THE NEWLY PLANTED TREE

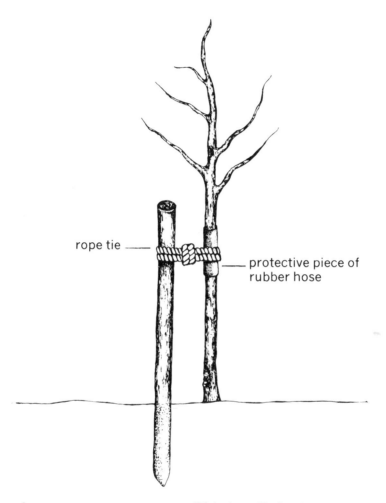

rope tie ——

—— protective piece of
rubber hose

the tree may sprout roots. This is called scion-rooting—
and since only the bottom, or root part of the tree, is the
dwarfing part, you'd eventually find yourself with a so-
called dwarf 30 or 40 feet high.

Trees dwarfed with stempieces are an exception to
this planting-depth procedure. As the illustration shows,
the graft union of a stempiece tree is a swelling on the
trunk, high enough so that the tree can usually be plant-

ed a little deeper than it grew in the nursery without any danger of scion-rooting.

Next, put enough topsoil-compost mixture into the hole to make a mound on which you can place the tree at the correct depth, with its roots spread out along the sides of the mound. Now fill in all but the top third of the hole, punching the earth down firmly with a hoe handle. This is also the moment to set a stake to support the young tree for its first three or four years while it is growing a strong root anchorage. As the illustration shows, the stake is set close to the tree (and can be closer than shown), and should be on the side the prevailing wind comes from. The trunk is then tied to the stake. Rope makes a good tie, and it is best to protect the trunk first with a sleeve of old garden hose.

Before filling in the rest of the hole with soil, pour in one or two buckets of water or compost solution. This is to settle the soil, getting rid of any air pockets that could dry out some roots. Compost solution is made by soaking about two spadefuls of compost in a bucket of water for an hour.

Next, fill in the hole completely, and build a low circular rim of earth all around the tree to form a 30-inch-wide basin. This is to hold water, as you may need to water the tree a few times if the season is dry. Don't overdo it, though, or you'll hurt the young roots. A mulch will help a lot here, keeping the earth moist. We will go into this further in the next chapter.

The next step is to protect the trunk from sunscald, from drying out, from borers and from animal nibbling. A simple way to do all this in one swoop is to wrap an 18-inch-wide strip of heavy-duty aluminum foil around the trunk, with the bottom 2 inches of the foil underground. Some people use old nylon stockings for trunk wrapping. After trees have grown old enough to have toughened their bark against sun damage, you can put a cylinder of hardware cloth around the trunk as a good barrier against animals, especially mice and rabbits in winter. Allow a few inches of space between the hardware cloth and the trunk. There is also a flexible metal strip that you wrap around the trunk like a puttee legging; it expands as needed, so does not bind the trunk.

THE FIRST PRUNING

Given their choice, we'd guess that 99 out of 100 new home fruit gardeners would not prune their fruit trees at all when planting them. A young fruit tree usually has several branches, called laterals, growing from the central stem, and it looks ambitious and complete, eager to show the world what it can do. Well, you don't *have to* prune this young tree. It will grow up just the same, and will bear fruit. So why prune it? For two excellent reasons. First, dormant-season pruning is a growth stimulant, and you do want the little tree to grow well. Second, this initial pruning is to establish the shape of the tree for life. If you allowed it to grow unpruned, it would develop into a thicket, the gloomy interior of which no ray of sunlight could kiss, and the result would be inferior fruit and a management headache for you.

As to tools, a scissors-action hand pruner will do everything you need done right now. Later a pair of loppers and a pruning saw will be convenient for cutting larger limbs.

Dwarf fruit trees are grown in either of two shapes:

1. Cone shape, in which a central trunk is surrounded by lateral limbs, the longer ones further down on the trunk, the shorter ones toward the top.

CONE SHAPE PRUNING AT PLANTING TIME—
APPLE, PEAR, EUROPEAN AND DAMSON PLUMS,
CHERRIES.

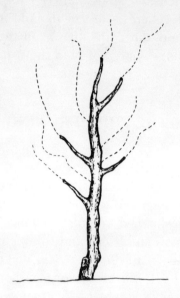

2. Vase shape, in which three or four lateral
limbs at about the same height, curve outward
and upward from the upper part of the short
trunk.

Here is how it is done for the fruits we are talking
about.

Apples: *Cone shape*

As shown in the illustration, select from three to five
good lateral branches that are well-spaced from each
other around and up and down the trunk. Prune these to
about 10 inches long. Next, prune back the central trunk
to about 12 inches from the point at which the highest
lateral branch that you are keeping connects with the
trunk. Then prune away entirely all other branches.

Make clean cuts with sharp pruners. It is not necessary to paint the cuts.

Apple trees dwarfed with stempieces, especially the

VASE SHAPE PRUNING AT PLANTING TIME—
PEACH, NECTARINE, APRICOT AND JAPANESE PLUM

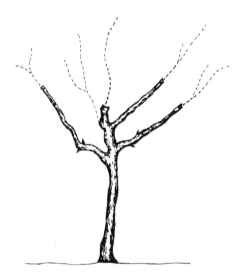

Stark double-dwarfs, can be pruned higher than trees dwarfed on the EM 9 rootstock; the EM 9 ones should have their lowest limbs about a foot from the ground. This is because their root anchorage is less strong and the trees need some help to keep from being blown over when young; retaining the low-growing limbs lowers the tree's center of gravity.

Pears: *Cone shape*

Prune the same as stempiece apples.

Peaches and Nectarines: *Vase shape*

Cut back the central trunk to about 2 feet above

ground level. Select three to five lateral branches that are well-spaced around the trunk and at similar heights on the trunk. Prune off about one third of each such lateral. Remove all other branches.

If the lateral branches you need are not very sturdy-looking, just prune them back hard—to stubs as long as your finger, leaving two or three buds on each. This will make them grow into stronger laterals.

European and Damson Plums: *Cone shape*

Prune the same as stempiece apple trees.

Japanese Plums: *Vase shape*

Prune as you do peaches.

Cherries: *Cone shape*

Prune as you do stempiece apple trees. If the young trees have no lateral branches yet, just prune back the top third of the central trunk.

Apricots: *Vase shape*

Prune as you do peaches.

COMPOST

No garden should be without a continuous supply of compost, and a fruit garden is no exception. Compost does three things for a garden: It improves soil texture, it conserves soil moisture, and it supplies fertilizer to plants. And making compost adds much to a gardener's sense of accomplishment.

If you are new at gardening, you may be wondering what exactly compost is. It is organic matter, usually garden and kitchen waste, that has been decomposed by bacteria and fungi. Good compost is a complete fertilizer, possessing all the nutrients plants need from the soil. Leaf mold is one kind of compost, and it accumulates on a forest floor without anyone's doing anything about it— so you can see from this that compost-making is a natural process and no mystery, except as nature's workings are always mysterious.

To make compost, you do much as nature does in the forest, which is to pile plant material on the ground. This sounds over-simplified, but it is literally true that if you did nothing else but this, you would in time have compost. However, since gardeners are an impatient lot and want compost faster than this beautifully easy way would provide it, they have worked out quicker ways. We'll describe two of them: The layer method and the turning method.

Layer Method

This is slower-acting but takes less work than the turning method. Start by chopping with a spade vegetable peelings, non-woody prunings, discarded vegetables, etc. into about 2-inch lengths. You can also include wood shavings, torn-up newspapers, grass clippings, coffee grounds, leaves, faded flowers, etc. We don't recommend fats, eggshells, stale bread, and the like because these will attract animals, but almost any soft vegetative waste will do.

Make a layer of this material on the ground, 6 inches thick. Put a 2-inch layer of earth on it. Repeat these layers, building up the pile to a convenient height, 3 to 5 feet, and about this same width and length. You can use a simple bin to keep the pile in place, but it isn't necessary. As you make the pile, wet the layers if they feel dry to the touch. They should feel damp-sponge moist. Finish off the top with a final layer of earth, and make a shallow basin in it to catch rain.

.

A compost pile made like this will decompose during a summer. In cold weather it will take six months or more. Repiling it once or twice will speed it up some, and will help the outer parts of the original pile to decompose at the same rate as the rest.

Turning Method

You can make compost in two weeks by this method. All you need are the same vegetative wastes we mentioned for use with the layer method. Earth isn't necessary, though it is all right to include some. The only real difference is in the handling. With the turning method, you chop up and pile the waste matter in a heap or bin, wetting it if necessary—and then for two weeks, you repile it every other day. At each repiling you try to put the outer material on the inside of the new pile. Add water if necessary, and see that the heap is compact (not springy), but not so compact that air can't get to the center of the pile. If the material isn't soggy wet, the pile probably won't be too compact.

The reason for needing the air penetration is that the bacteria you want to encourage are the kind that need air, so-called aerobic bacteria. You don't have to add them, or anything else, to the organic materials. The bacteria are already on the materials, and the fungi that enter into the decomposition also appear at the right time.

As decomposition proceeds, the pile will heat up and will be steaming by the first or second turnings. Temperatures will run up to about 160° F. in a well-handled pile, and in fact the organic material will soon look as if it's been cooked.

This compost, or that from the layer method, is ready to use when it has turned dark, smells something like forest earth, and when you can no longer recognize the things that went into it—except for tough stems, which take two or three compostings to tame.

We like to use a low bin to hold the heap when we make compost by the turning method, and we have found we can make it in smaller quantities than you usually see recommended. Instead of a heap 3 to 5 feet high and square, we make one 2 to 3 feet high and square. It decomposes just as fast, so we can have finished compost by the time we would merely have accumulated enough material for a bigger heap.

If you have a shredder, it will save work in hand-chopping the raw material of compost, but don't shred it too fine or you'll have trouble keeping air inside the heap. Studies have shown that a 2-inch length for most materials is about right.

We strongly recommend that you keep a compost heap going along all the time. Compost is a good mulch for any plant, but for dwarf fruit trees it is ideal, as it also feeds the trees. In this sense it is a slow-release fertilizer, so that a compost mulch can be applied immediately after the trees are planted, even though little or no fertilizer is required at that time. We'll have more to say about compost from time to time further on.

3

The Second
and Future Years

You now have your dwarf trees going along, their first
year successfully behind them, and you and they stand
on the threshhold of the second year and all the years to
come. This is a solid part of the really satisfying life, and
we envy you this first-time taste of it. Fruit gardening
has been the pleasure and pastime of monarchs, but none
of them ever possessed so fine a little tree as the newest
dwarfs that are yours to enjoy and tend.

In this chapter we will take up the care of your trees
as they settle into their growing-up and producing years.
Dwarf trees mature quickly, so that the second-year care
is much the same as the attention you will be paying
them each year hereafter.

For the sake of keeping matters in order, we'll begin
with pruning because it is the first thing you do for your
trees as the year begins to unfold. Following this month-
by-month timing in a general way, we will take up these
other items in this order: pest control, fertilizing, frost
control, watering and mulching, and fruit thinning. The

final step, harvesting, is going to be covered in the next chapter, fruit by fruit.

PRUNING

The winter pruning, the first item each year on the gardening season's calendar, is done as soon as the worst of the winter cold is over, from January or even a month before in warm climates, to April in cold ones. As we said in the previous chapter, you would get fruit even if you never pruned your dwarf trees, but by doing some pruning you'll get better growth and better-shaped trees, and this means more fruit and better fruit.

But it is better to do too little pruning rather than too much. Overpruning will starve a tree and reduce the harvest. The trees that take the most pruning (and can be pruned a little later than others) are peaches, nectarines, and apricots. Of the others, the pear takes least.

To get down to brass tacks, there are only two basic choices when you decide to prune a tree limb. They are: Should you cut the limb completely off? Or should you cut it only partly off? You cut it completely off if: it is dead; it is growing out at a poor angle (too upright, usually); it is hurting the shape of the tree; it is a sucker springing up from the roots; or it is a watersprout—a vertical limb in the tree's interior.

You cut a limb partly off to control fruit production and tree form, and this is by far the most common pruning. When you cut part of a limb off, you can be sure of one thing—the leaf bud nearest the cut end will be determined to grow and extend the limb once more, as if bent on undoing your work. You can't stop the bud from growing, so what you do is to make your cut just short of a leaf bud that is *pointing in the direction you want the new growth to go*. Simple? In such ways do we outfox Mother Nature by letting her do what she is bound to do anyway.

Notice that we said you cut back to just short of

BUDS

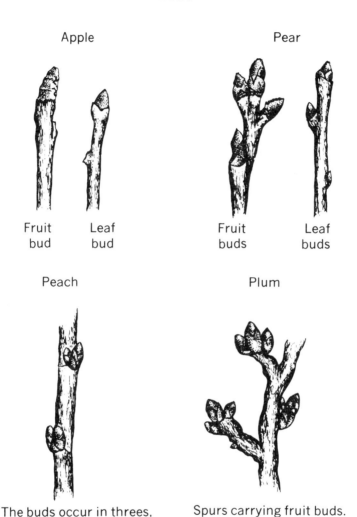

Apple

Fruit   Leaf
bud   bud

Pear

Fruit   Leaf
buds   buds

Peach

The buds occur in threes,
a leaf bud between two
fruit buds.

Plum

Spurs carrying fruit buds.

(within about ¼-inch of) a *leaf* bud. The only other kind of bud is a flower bud. You can tell them apart by their shape. Both are found here and there on branches and trunks, tightly folded little bumps with pointed ends. But, as the illustration shows, a flower bud is always plump, and a leaf bud is slender. A leaf bud always grows into wood and leaves, and a flower bud becomes the flower that then grows into the fruit. Of the fruits we are covering in this book, all except peaches and nectarines bear their flower buds on short twigs called spurs. Even peaches and nectarines may have a few spurs, but you'll find that most of their flower buds lie close against their slender outer branches, usually a pair of flower buds with a leaf bud between them.

Needless to say, sharp tools are the rule in pruning. Not only do they make the job easier and more interesting, but a clean cut heals fast, while a ragged one invites pest invasion. With dwarf trees, the cut ends are seldom big enough to need a protective coating, but if you don't like the raw look of the cut, use Tree Seal, an asphalt preparation that we like, or a water-soluble tree paint, both carried by garden centers.

If you have to cut into diseased wood, sterilize your pruner between cuts by dipping the blades into rubbing alcohol or into a half-and-half solution of liquid laundry bleach and water.

By their third year your dwarf trees will have settled into their proper shape, and your pruning from then on should be as little as possible to maintain good shape and good fruiting—as explained below for each fruit.

Apples

After the first season's growth, the next spring's pruning consists of retaining from four to nine or so good framework branches, and removing others. The criteria for good framework branches is that they be well spaced from each other both up and down the trunk and around it, and that they form wide, not narrow, angles with the trunk. A 60-degree angle is about right, which is two thirds of the way toward a perfectly horizontal position.

After selecting these framework branches and removing the others, prune the framework ones back by a third

MATURE CONE SHAPE—APPLE, PEAR,
EUROPEAN AND DAMSON PLUMS, CHERRIES

or even a half. This kind of pruning-back can be repeated the following year as well. The object is to force the tree into a compact growth in which fruit will be borne close to the trunk. This makes a stronger tree, able to carry a heavier load of fruit.

From this point on, comparatively little pruning is needed for dwarf apple trees. Just remove dead wood and any branches that are crowding others or are poorly shaped. In this way you keep good new wood growing, and this gives you more fruit per tree.

Pears

Dwarf pears are trained into the central leader, or cone, form, like apples. Follow the instructions given for apples, but if your pear trees grow too strongly, simply head back terminal shoots enough to maintain a good shape of tree. After the trees are four or five years old they will become docile in this respect and will keep their proper shape without much effort on your part.

Peaches and Nectarines

The vase shape is the right one here, so you keep pruning to develop it, formed by the upward-reaching lateral branches you have retained after your pruning at planting time. Peach and nectarine trees are vigorous growers, and need more pruning than the other fruits. They bear their fruit on wood they have grown the season before. This wood is farthest out on the branches at the end of its growing season, of course. During the following spring pruning, about a third or half of this new wood should be cut back on each of the branches. This must be done every spring, to keep the tree from growing gawky, and also to keep it from bearing too many fruits (in which case they would all be small unless you spent a great deal of effort thinning them; your pruning, you see, is also a fruit-thinning operation).

And, as with other fruit trees, keep the interior of peach and nectarine trees open to sunlight by removing interferring shoots.

After a peach or nectarine tree is a few years old, some of the branches will have grown too long, due to their habit of growing a little longer each year in order to produce new fruit-bearing wood. The remedy for these too-long branches is ruthlessness. You prune them hard, heading them back to some convenient point where a good lateral branch occurs. This will throw strength into the lateral. It is a sort of hair-cut procedure, sprucing up the looks of the tree as well as helping the crop.

Plums

As noted in Chapter 2, at planting time the European and Damson plums are pruned like the apple, to grow into the cone shape. Japanese plums, however, do best when pruned like peaches, to the vase shape.

All three species of plums have the habit of becoming pretty thickety by growing lots of short branches in the interiors of the trees. This isn't a good habit because it keeps sunlight from entering and complicates harvesting and other husbandry. The remedy is simple, though: Merely snip out surplus twiggy growth, and *don't* head back the tips of framework branches any more than you have to. The reason for this caution is that any such heading-back is apt to throw the tree into a burst of twigginess.

Plum trees are generally agreeable creatures, but if an older tree becomes uninterested in bearing good crops, try this: Head back a few of the older limbs to the point at which good outward-pointing branches join them. This will cause a growth of new shoots, and you can then choose the best of them to keep.

Cherries

As we mentioned briefly in Chapter 2, sour cherries usually need little pruning once they are established. Just clip off any terminal growth that may get out of hand, and keep the interior of the tree open by removing any shoots that threaten to crowd it and keep sunlight out. There is always a certain amount of dead wood to be removed each season from cherry trees.

Sweet cherries take the same attention, but more of

it. They are stronger growers than sour cherry trees, and so in the second and future seasons may need more heading-back of branches and more thinning of unwanted branches.

If either class of cherry slows down in its production, treat it as described for the unthrifty plum tree.

Apricots

Apricots are pruned to vase shape, like peaches, and the pruning is much like that given to peaches.

Since apricots bear their fruit on spurs that live for about three years, you might think that the peach-pruning technique of shortening the branches would prune off too many spurs to set a good crop. This is not so, for two reasons: Apricots are very vigorous growers and would get too thickety if not pruned more severely than other trees that grow fruit on spurs; and this hard pruning makes the apricot trees form *new* spurs at a great rate because you let sunshine into the tree interior when you remove older wood. The branches to remove are the thinner, weaker ones, and the ones that are crowding others.

PEST CONTROL

When it comes to doing something about pests, which means insects and diseases, home gardeners fall into one of three groups: chemical, organic, or compromise. We make a point of including the compromise group because we have noticed that many home gardeners fall into this group on pest control only.

Today, a chemical-control home gardener will do most or all of his pest-fighting with a combination chemical spray, one that includes one or more insecticides, a miticide, and one or two fungicides. A frequently found combination is that of malathion, methoxychlor, and captan. There are many brands on the market using this

MATURE VASE SHAPE—PEACH, NECTARINE,
APRICOT, JAPANESE PLUM

or a comparable mix, and the home fruit gardener who employs one of them will put about a quart of spray on each of his trees four to six times a season, following a schedule on the package of spray.

An organic-control gardener wouldn't touch this combination spray with a 10-foot pole, but will choose among various non-chemical controls, some of which are homemade and some commercial. We describe the chief such controls a little further along.

The compromise-control home gardener is organic as long as he feels the pests aren't too bad. If he decides they are becoming too big a threat he hits the panic button and slaughters them with a chemical spray.

None of the three groups has so far been able to prove to the others that its method is unquestionably best, and there is much argument among them. However, the organic-control method offers the hope of an eventual true harmony with nature—a most telling point today and a consummation devoutly to be wished.

But at this writing the only reasonable approach to no-poison pest control is to regard yourself as a pioneer and experimenter. *Somebody* has to keep trying out alternatives to poisons, and you can safely bet anything you please that the average commercial operator won't try them—in fact, can't—because fruit growing is a living with him, and he'd go broke if non-poisonous controls didn't work well for him or didn't work soon enough. And the risk that they *wouldn't* work soon enough is high. It is common experience with home gardeners that the first season they garden purely organically, the pests are worse than ever. It is not until the second or third year that, given an increasingly healthy soil, close owner-attention, and a buildup of the many helpful insects (no longer being killed along with the bad ones with poisons), results show up in the form of fruits with less and less damage.

Although there are almost no varieties of fruits resistant to insect attacks, some varieties are resistant to certain diseases. One big nursery, Stark Bro's, makes a point of telling its organic customers which of its trees are especially disease-resistant. In dwarf sizes these include Starkspur Golden Delicious apple—resistant to scab, cedar rust, blotch, and blight; Starkspur EarliBlaze apple—resistant to scab, mildew, and blotch; Early White Giant peach—resistant to scab and bacterial spot; Starking Delicious pear and Moonglow pear—resistant to scab and fire blight. It is always a good idea to plant a variety resistant to a disease if the disease is prevalent in your area. The best way to check for such prevalence is to ask your county agent.

Sanitation is the next step in pest control. Keep any diseased wood pruned out of your trees—and do this pruning as soon as you see diseased wood. Also keep dead wood pruned out. Remove and destroy wormy fruit, and remove any dried-up fruit left hanging on the trees at the end of the season. Keep prunings cleaned up, and burn them. Keep fallen leaves cleaned up—some fungi live over the winter on fallen leaves. Keep weeds down—curculio beetles like to hide in weedy corners. Prune to keep the interior of your trees open to sun and air, and this includes the removal of watersprouts when they spring up in early summer.

When you find a cluster of insect eggs on a leaf or around a twig, crush them. One easily recognizable exception is the tiny egg borne on the tip of a tiny stalk placed on the upper surface of a leaf. This is the egg of a lacewing fly, a valuable predator of many harmful insects.

In addition to choosing resistant varieties and paying attention to sanitation, keeping your trees in vigorous health will go a long way toward pest control. The healthy tree is always a growthy one, and tree health depends on good management practices—proper site for air and sun; good drainage; fertilizing and watering when needed—all the things, in fact, that we take up in this book, plus always your personal interest in your trees, for nothing takes the place of this.

And, by the way, keep a garden diary, noting in it what pests showed up during a year, when they did, what you did about it and how well it worked. Such a record will be a big help to you in future seasons—remember that forewarned is forearmed.

We would like to mention one way that some home gardeners prevent damage to pears and apples, peaches and nectarines, though it does take some doing. They fasten a paper bag around each fruit, stapling the bag together at the top to hold it on, and cutting off the bottom corners to let any moisture drain out. The bags are put on quite early in the season after the fruit are formed, and are not taken off until harvest time. It seems to be a Japanese idea, and seems to work well.

Since we don't cover repellents below, we'll say a word about them here. Organic gardeners who refuse to use any insecticide, even those that are plant-derived, such as rotenone, often rely on repellents to keep insects away. The variety of repellents is wonderful, including sea water, solutions of various weeds, and perfumed mixtures. We have a notion that sometimes the repellent gets credit for what something else is doing—but in general our feeling is, if it seems to work for you, fine.

Pests

Following the description of each insect or disease, we give various controls. Use one or more of these, as needed.

Aphids

Also called plant lice, these are small, soft, pear-shaped insects of various colors. They suck juices from stems and leaves, working in colonies and multiplying rapidly, especially in warm, dry weather. Damage is shown by distorted and discolored leaves. The effect is to weaken the tree.

Control ants (which protect aphids).

Encourage ladybugs (which eat aphids).

Spray with a strong stream of plain water.

Spray with a soap solution: 1/3 cup "green soap" from the drug store in 1 gallon of water; wash it off before it dries on the tree.

Spray with nicotine sulfate, with rotenone, or with ryania.

Dust with Perma-Guard.

Crush aphids by hand.

In early spring before buds open and on a day when the temperature is above 50° F., use a 3% miscible oil dormant spray, or a 2% "superior oil" dormant spray; or use a kerosene solution (2 tablespoons kerosene, 1 cup soap flakes, 1 gallon water).

Apple maggots

These are the larvae of a fly that looks much like a house fly. In July and August maggots hatch from eggs that the fly deposits on fruit, usually on apples, but cherries and European plums are also vulnerable. The maggots tunnel into the fruit, making winding passages, and "railroad worm" is another term for this pest.

Prevention is the best control. During August and September, keep gathering all fallen fruit, as any maggots in them will burrow into the soil and come out the next year as flies. It is also helpful to run poultry in the orchard, and to keep weeds cleaned out.

During the summer, trap flies in Mason jars hung in the trees, the jar openings covered with hardware cloth, and the jars half filled with this solution: 1 cup of molasses, 1 tablespoon dry yeast, 1 gallon of water.

Apple scab

This is a fungus disease that shows up as velvety olive-green spots on leaves, twigs, and fruit.

Dust with wettable sulfur, or spray with it, 3 tablespoons to 1 gallon of water, in early spring before blossoms open. Repeat after petals fall, and again 10 days later if the season is wet.

Birds

Although birds destroy many harmful insects, the birds also eat a good deal of fruit, being especially avid for cherries.

A practical way for a home fruit gardener to protect his trees is with nylon mesh sold for this purpose. See chapter 10.

Black knot

Plums and cherries—especially if the trees have been neglected—may get this fungus disease. It appears on the wood as greenish knots that then turn black. Cut out and burn the knots promptly, preferably while they are still green.

Borers

These are worms that tunnel into the tree trunk near ground level, and into limbs. Their presence is signaled by gum forming at the hole where they enter. Peach trees are their favorites, but nectarine, plum, cherry, and apricot trees are all vulnerable.

Run a wire into the hole to destroy the borer, or cut it out with a knife.

Prevent entry by painting trunks with a thin paste of wood ashes and water.

Prevent entry by wrapping trunks with masking tape, from 3 inches below ground level to 4 inches above it, replacing dug-out soil when done.

Fasten bars of homemade lye soap to trunks

just below lowest branches, so rain can wash a soapy runoff into the ground.

Band trunks with Tanglefoot. (Paint the bands the next spring with turpentine to renew their stickiness for another season.)

Brown rot

Attacking stone fruits, especially in wet seasons, this fungus disease causes decay of peaches, nectarines, plums, cherries, and apricots.

Prevention is the only way to handle this problem. Spray with wettable sulfur, 3 tablespoons to 1 gallon of water, before fruits start to ripen.

Keep windfalls cleaned up, and gather and destroy any shrunken, dried fruits on the trees.

To prevent development of brown rot in stored fruits, put them in 140° F. water for two minutes after harvesting.

Codling moth

This is the adult form of the apple worm, the apple's commonest pest. The moth is ½ inch long, brownish-gray, and the worm is ¼ inch long and pinkish.

In early spring before buds open, use an oil spray (*see Aphids*).

To destroy cocoons and break pest cycle, scrape loose bark off trunk in spring, burn scrapings, and scrub trunk with soapy water.

Trap worms under burlap or cotton batting bands which have been wrapped around trunk and wadded in crotches, and destroy them.

Dust with Perma-Guard.

Band trunks with Tanglefoot (*see Borers*).

Keep windfalls cleaned up.

Trap moths in jars of molasses solution (*see Apple Maggots*).

Spray with ryania, 1 tablespoon of 100% dust to 1 gallon of water, as follows: 10 days after the petals fall; three more times at 10-day intervals; then again when the second brood of worms hatch (check this date for your locality with your county agent).

Note: Trichogramma wasps destroy eggs of codling moth and of some other pests; although most home gardeners will not find it practical to purchase this form of control, the chances are fair that these little wasps are already present in their areas.

Curculio beetles

Also called plum curculio, the larva of this pest is the trouble-maker, a worm that invades fruits of apple, plum, cherry, apricot, nectarine, and sometimes peach.

Band trunks with Tanglefoot (*see Borers*).

Run chickens under the trees, and shake beetles loose from branches.

Fire blight

Caused by bacteria, this disease shows up as blackened, burned-looking branches on apple and pear trees. It has been with us for 200 years and there is no cure as yet, although there are resistant varieties of fruits.

Immediately on seeing a blighted branch, remove and destroy it; breaking it off is better than waiting until you have a pruning shears at hand; you can prune the broken stub smoothly later.

Reduce fertilizing, as new growth is most susceptible to blight.

Japanese beetles

These oval, green-and-brown ½-inch-long beetles sometimes eat leaves and fruits of trees, while their grub larvae eat roots, but they are not the menace they were a few years ago.

Break the life cycle by treating the soil with spores of milky disease (Bug Doom is one brand name) to kill the larvae.

Kill any grubs found when spading soil.

Protect trees with netting (*see Birds*).

Spray with rotenone or ryania during any serious attack.

Leaf-curl

This common fungus disease of peach and nectarine trees shows up in early spring as distorted and discolored leaves that then fall; this leaf loss weakens the tree, reducing or eliminating the crop.

Prevention is the proper procedure. In early spring or late winter before any buds show green, spray the trees with wettable sulfur, 3 tablespoons to 1 gallon of water.

If only a few leaves are affected, remove and burn them.

If most leaves are affected, remove and burn them, then give the trees a nitrogen boost by working twice as much blood meal into the soil as suggested for normal spring feeding (to be discussed later in this chapter).

Mites

These are tiny sucking insects (or, technically, arachnids) that attack apple trees and sometimes other fruit trees. The leaves turn bronze and yellow, and then fall.

Prevention is the best course; in early spring before any buds show green, use an oil spray (*see Aphids*).

If mites are present, coat and kill them with this spray: 1 cup of flour, 2 tablespoons of buttermilk, and enough water to make a thin paste, in 1 gallon of water.

Dust with Perma-Guard.

Oriental fruit moth

The larvae, small pink worms, work their way into the tips of peach twigs and into the fruits.

Prevention is the proper procedure. In early spring before buds show green, use an oil spray (*see Aphids*).

Pear Psylla

This aphid-like sucking insect, about 1/10 inch long, reveals itself by the blackish fungus that forms on a sticky deposit the psylla makes on leaves.

Remove the fungus by swabbing affected leaves with a damp cloth.

Spray insects with nicotine sulfate.

For prevention, use an oil spray in early spring before buds show green (*see Aphids*).

Rabbits

Because they gnaw bark, rabbits can girdle and kill a young fruit tree.

In Chapter 2 we suggested various ways to protect the trunk. Another measure, though a temporary one, is to spray trunks with a solution of 1 tablespoon of dried blood to 1 gallon of water. This is also a mild nitrogenous fertilizing.

Scale

These are sucking insects of various kinds. In most cases, they work under tiny individual shell-like coverings. They attack apple trees and fruits, and sometimes peach, sweet cherry, and apricot trees.

In early spring, before buds show green, use an oil spray (*see Aphids*).

With a wad of burlap, rub off the tree any colonies of scales.

Web caterpillars

These caterpillars show up as colonies encased in webs something like spider webs, netted around bunches of leaves at the far ends of branches. Though more troublesome with nut trees, they sometimes attack fruit trees. With dwarf trees, control is not difficult.

In winter, search out the egg masses on trees —lumpy gray wads—and burn them.

During the growing season, prune off and burn the branch tips holding webs; do this at the end of the day, when the feeding caterpillars will have returned to their webs for the night.

Band trunk with Tanglefoot (*see Borers*).

Yellow-leaf

This fungus disease of plums and sometimes of cherries turns leaves yellowish, and they then fall, weakening the tree.

Break the cycle by keeping fallen leaves, on which spores over-winter, cleaned up and burned.

FERTILIZING

If you have planted your dwarf trees in fertile soil they will be getting most or all the nutrients they need without your help. Fruit trees are good at mining the soil, and it is astonishing how they can make bushels of apples or whatever, out of practically nothing. Or so it seems from a gardener's-eye view.

But a dwarf tree, we must admit, is not as well equipped with roots for food foraging as a large fruit tree is. Also, the dwarf is a more efficient producer, putting proportionately more units of its total energy into fruits than the large tree does. Consequently, a dwarf fruit tree can usually use fertilizing if it is to do its best.

A good deal of personal judgment goes into the fertilizing programs used by experienced fruit gardeners, and when you have lived with your own trees for a while you'll find yourself doing the same thing—adding more fertilizer if your trees seem to need a boost, or reducing fertilizing if they seem over-stimulated, especially in leaf growth. The fertilizers we speak of below are slow-release kinds, and the amounts given are moderate.

The fertilizing program we suggest consists of only two materials: blood meal, and compost. Fertilizing is ordinarily done only once a year, in very early spring or in late winter. Some gardeners like to give a second fertilizing to their trees in the fall after growth has stopped for the year. We prefer a single fertilizing early in the year, however. Remember also that fruit trees that get more fertilizer than they need will waste it by growing more twigs and leaves than they know what to do with, and such trees are also more subject to injury from winter cold.

In late winter or early spring, then—say from December to April, depending on your climate—give each dwarf *apple* or *pear* tree one cup of blood meal. This amount is intended for trees between about three and ten years old. Younger trees will need only about ½ cup of blood meal, and trees older than ten years will need up to two cups of blood meal. For the stone fruits—*peach, nectarine, plum, cherry,* and *apricot*—give half again as much blood meal per tree: ¾ cup for young trees, 1½ cups for those three to ten years old, and 3 cups for older trees.

Spread the blood meal from within 1 foot of the trunk, out to 1 foot farther than the branches reach, and work it into the ground with shallow cultivation. If you are keeping a mulch on the ground, as recommended, rake the mulch aside before spreading the blood meal, and work the blood meal into the soil with a rake.

Follow this blood meal application with a compost application. A conservative amount of compost to use is about one bucketful per tree. Give young trees half as much, and older trees twice as much. In our experience, fruit trees welcome compost, and we have sometimes given them double or triple these amounts.

In case you are mulching your trees with compost,

this should supply all the fertilizing they will need, and you can omit the blood meal.

You can also omit the blood meal if your trees seem to be growing a great many leaves but not much fruit, as this is a sign of too much nitrogen, in which blood meal is rich.

If you don't have a compost program going, or if you simply don't have enough compost to go around when fertilizing time comes, use the blood meal in the quantities suggested, and add double those amounts of cottonseed meal, soybean meal, or linseed meal.

FROST CONTROL

Late spring is a nervous time for a home fruit gardener (and for commercial growers as well) because of the frost danger. The early spring frosts are seldom troublesome, but a late and hard frost can mean no fruit that season. If it is any comfort, this gives a tree a summer vacation and you can look forward to a bigger harvest the following year. But what you really want is a harvest every year from every tree, including peaches, nectarines, and apricots—the three most apt to be nipped by frost because they are always in a great hurry to bloom. So, although frost damage can always be regarded philosophically as an act of God, in this case heaven often helps those who help themselves, if they are quick about it.

Our own brushes with frost move us to recommend four frost foilers to you: windbreaks, water, coverings, and fans. A fifth, and one much used commercially, is heat, but we have never thought this practical for a home gardener unless he is a one-tree gardener and wants to put a tent over his baby when frost threatens, and a light bulb on an outdoor extension cord hung inside a bucket in the tent.

The idea of a windbreak is to keep strong winds from adding to the damage that cold can cause. If you plant your trees near your house or other buildings, these will act as windbreaks if they are between the trees and the prevailing wind. A board fence makes a good and quickly built windbreak. Set the boards in louvred formation, like venetian blind slats on end, so that some wind can get through and provide needed ventilation at other seasons of the year. A hedge of evergreens makes an excellent windbreak. Start it a year or two before planting your fruit trees, or provide a temporary fence windbreak while the evergreen one is growing up.

Water is one of the best frost fighters. By spraying the trees with a hose early in the morning when frost is present, you have a chance of stopping frost damage. You can also help by wetting down the planting before frost is expected, say during the previous afternoon. Water helps prevent frost damage in two ways:

1. As it evaporates, it raises the capacity of the air to absorb heat and this heat can be released later, protecting the trees.

2. As the water cools, it gives off heat, quite a bit; a mere two gallons of water in chilling down 30 degrees will release as much warmth as a 500-watt heater puts out in 15 minutes.

Covering the trees when frost is expected is an old and a good way to protect them. In fact, in a light frost the trees do this for themselves somewhat, the lower blossoms being protected by growth in the upper parts of the tree where blossoms are apt to be killed by the cold. If the spring day has been warmer than normal, and if the night is clear and calm but chills off rapidly, be prepared with old sheets, canvas, burlap, paper drop cloths, or whatever you have that is big enough to drape over your little trees—and get them covered soon after sundown if not earlier. The covering should touch the ground if possible, to hold in the earth heat, which is being lost with every passing minute after dark. It will help a little more if you can turn the hose on the trees before covering them.

In England some commercial fruit growers have experimented successfully with a plastic mesh covering that they stretch over a framework, covering the entire orchard. A framework support is a good idea, but most home gardeners feel lucky if they merely have enough coverings quickly at hand to fling over their trees.

After suggesting windbreaks to you as frost protection, it may seem peculiar that another form of protection we now suggest is wind itself, through the use of a fan. However, moving the air by setting a window fan where it will blow through the trees is one way some home gardeners foil frost. It has worked for us, or at least we think it helped. The way this frost-foiler operates is by mingling colder low-lying air with warmer and higher air. This may work if there isn't much wind. If, however, the wind is strong on a frosty night, it will be bringing in cold air, and stirring the cold air with a fan won't buy you anything in that case.

WATERING AND MULCHING

We are taking these two subjects up together because they are so intertwined. In fact, you won't have to trouble your head about watering your fruit trees if they are well mulched and if the rain doesn't desert you absolutely. And even in an extended drought you need not water dwarf fruit trees oftener than every two or three weeks if you keep a good mulch on them. (It is not only possible to *over*water a dwarf tree, it is often done by over-zealous gardeners who think a bucket a day keeps troubles away. Instead, it can kill the tree, in effect drowning the roots. The way to tell if a dwarf needs water is to see if its leaves are wilting.)

How much water do you give the tree, when you give it any? Give it the equal of a one-inch rain. This amount will penetrate 5 inches into average garden soil. You need not remove the mulch when you do this watering, and the mulch will even help by keeping the water from running off. If you are using a sprinkler you can measure the amount of water it is supplying by placing a few tin cans here and there around the area to see when they have caught about an inch of water. When setting the sprinkler, remember that the area you want to cover is roughly a foot or so farther out from the tree trunk than the longest branches.

Our preference for mulching trees is compost, for it feeds the tree as well as mulching it, and establishes a healthy soil environment at once. An exception, and a fairly rare one, would be a tree that could not take the feeding that compost would give it, thereby producing leaves at the expense of fruit. But most can use a compost mulch, and the only trouble is, this can take more compost than you may have. Well, cheer up—any mulch gradually turns into compost anyway. We mean any organic mulch; if you want to use sheet plastic for mulching, that's different. We like plastics for certain things but up to this time we haven't used plastic for mulching. If you try plastic mulch, keep in mind that it will *raise* soil temperatures in summer (the clear plastic more so than the dark plastic), whereas an organic mulch *lowers* them. And a Midwestern summer will boost soil temperature to well over 100° F. This is pretty warm for fruit tree roots near the surface, which dwarf-tree roots are. A temperature somewhere in the 70s suits them much better. In winter, the organic mulch keeps the soil a little warmer than if it were bare, which is also good.

Some other kinds of mulches are straw, sawdust, pine needles, wood shavings, ground-up corncobs, mushroom soil, grass clippings, and leaves. As you see, there is quite a variety. We have used weeds for mulching, as long as they weren't carrying seeds, and we've used old strawy stable manure when we had a lot of it, usually mixing it with some other mulch. Once, when we had to clean a lot of water weeds out of a pond we had, we used them as a mulch, and with a great deal of satisfaction at getting some use from the pesky things.

Some gardeners like to mulch with rocks because they keep the soil beneath them consistently moist, and they last forever. If you want to try rocks, use good-sized flat ones, and start out by spreading some other mulch such as leaves or sawdust on the ground first. You'll need to renew this under-mulch each year.

One point to keep firmly in mind about mulch is how close to the tree trunk it can come. It should clear the trunk by 6 to 12 inches all around, because if you nestle mulch right up against the trunk, the bark will become tender and therefore a greater temptation to mice, rabbits, borers, and other scoundrels. Also, a mulch close to the trunk gives the mice a good cover to hide under as they nibble the bark.

The depth of a mulch can vary a good deal, but 6 inches is a working average. The finer-textured the mulch is, the less depth you need. Sawdust will do a job for you when it is only 2 inches deep. So will grass clippings. Both these materials tend to mat, though, and make better mulches when mixed with shavings or some other such coarser material.

Any organic mulch will gradually settle, since it will be decomposing gradually, the way compost does. This is why you keep adding mulch each year. Actually, you are building soil, and very good soil.

You will often hear that you must add nitrogen when applying mulch, because as mulch decomposes, the bacteria doing this work require nitrogen, and will compete with tree roots for it in the soil. We find that with a succulent green mulch such as weeds this is true, and one cup of blood meal should be sprinkled over such a mulch around the tree. But mulches such as sawdust and shavings decompose so slowly that they need no nitrogen added, and doing so may overfeed the tree.

FRUIT THINNING

The first sight of fruit actually forming on dwarf trees is so heady that the new fruit gardener has a terrible tussle with himself about whether he will follow good advice and remove some of the fruits while they are still quite small—about the size shown in the drawings illustrating stages of fruit formation. Sometimes the best way to convince such a gardener that thinning, as fruit removal at this stage is called, is good practice is to let him alone to discover what happens when he doesn't thin.

When the tree is not fruit-thinned, the mature fruits are runty and poorly colored at harvest time. While every fruit tree drops some fruit voluntarily—the so-called June drop, though there are actually three drops during June—it still wants to bear more fruit than it can possibly support well. Here's how it works: A dwarf apple tree needs at least 25 leaves to grow one good big apple, and this is true in varying proportion with the other fruits. If the apple tree tries to support *two* apples with each set of 25 leaves, neither will be much of an apple. Therefore, we thin.

Also, thinning keeps a tree bearing annually, especially if it is one that would bear every other year if left to itself.

The way to thin is by hand. Just give the little green fruits a twist with your fingers, and pull them off; or hold them between thumb and forefinger while you snap them off with your middle finger. Because the upper parts of the tree have more slender limbs, do more thinning there than lower down. It is all right to leave enough fruits on the upper limbs to weigh the limbs down toward the hori-

STAGES OF FRUIT GROWTH (APPLES)

1. Pre-pink. Leaves formed, but buds show no color yet.

2. Buds now showing color.

3. Full bloom.

4. Small green fruits formed.

zontal as the season goes on. This is said to "umbrella" the tree, and the effect will be a tree that is permanently more fruitful and more dwarfed.

In general, do your thinning early in July (or a little sooner in warm areas). This gives the June drops a chance to do some of it for you, but yet gets it done soon enough for the tree to put all available nourishment into the fruits you let it keep.

Here are the general rules on how far apart fruits should be after you finish thinning. These are still very young fruits, remember, and when they mature they will be much closer than this, in many cases touching each other.

Apples and Pears	6 to 8 inches apart
Peaches and Nectarines	4 to 5 inches apart
Japanese plums	3 to 4 inches apart
European and Damson plums	usually no thinning needed
Cherries	no thinning needed
Apricots	3 to 4 inches apart

For a handy gauge that you can't possibly mislay, measure your fingers and your hand. A common hand length is about 6 inches, a finger is frequently about 3 inches long, and a finger joint, about an inch long.

4

The Fruits

A home gardener today has a marvelous choice of dwarf fruit trees—far wider than any commercial grower can consider. Leafing through the pages of this chapter, you can pick and choose from among nearly a hundred splendid little trees. There are still more of them in Chapter 7, which pays particular attention to collector's items, such as very old varieties and very choice ones; most of these are rarely offered any more. And in Chapter 8 you will find still another group, those especially for difficult climates.

In this present chapter we take up the fruits in this order: apples, pears, peaches, nectarines, plums, cherries, and apricots. We give some general cultural information for each, supplementing what was covered in the preceding chapters. Zone references are to the U.S. Department of Agriculture's Plant Hardiness Zone Map, but are only a general guide since there are countless local variations. For each fruit we list a number of good, available varieties in alphabetical order, and name the nurseries that

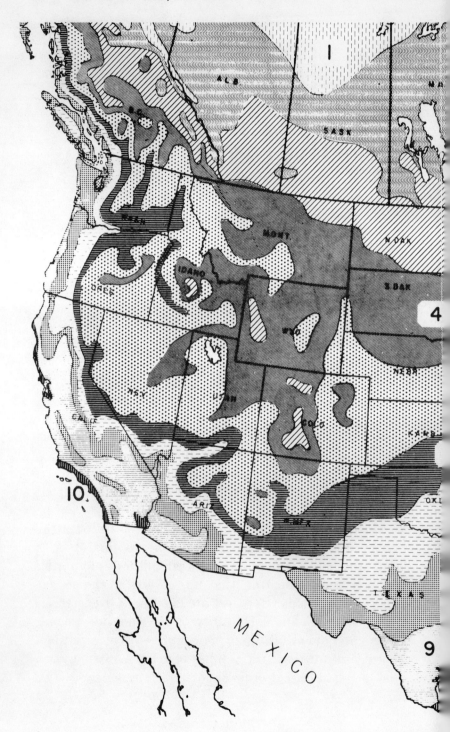

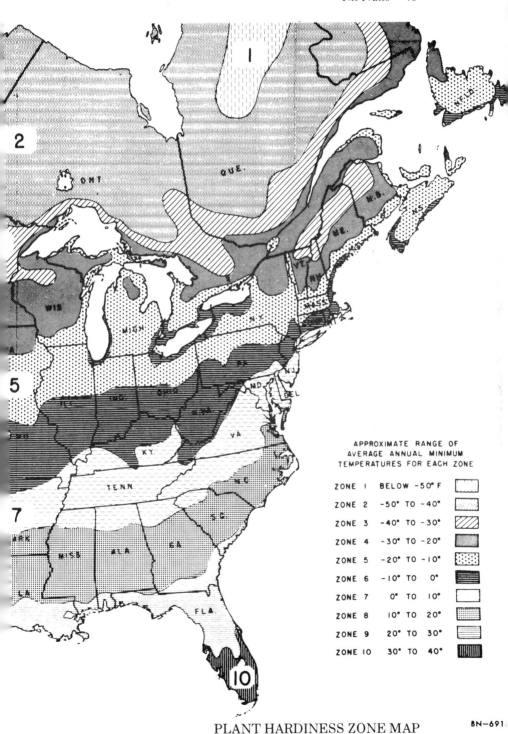

PLANT HARDINESS ZONE MAP

APPROXIMATE RANGE OF
AVERAGE ANNUAL MINIMUM
TEMPERATURES FOR EACH ZONE

ZONE 1	BELOW -50° F
ZONE 2	-50° TO -40°
ZONE 3	-40° TO -30°
ZONE 4	-30° TO -20°
ZONE 5	-20° TO -10°
ZONE 6	-10° TO 0°
ZONE 7	0° TO 10°
ZONE 8	10° TO 20°
ZONE 9	20° TO 30°
ZONE 10	30° TO 40°

BN-691

handle each variety; you will find the nurseries' full names and addresses in Chapter 10.

Each variety is described to help you choose the best for you among those your climate will suit—and it may be of interest here to say something about how fruits are described.

For many years professional horticulturists have used a standard vocabulary in telling each other what fruits taste like. In this way, everybody knows what everybody else means when he says a fruit is sour, or sweet. Though such descriptions are not exact, even when standard modifying terms are attached, they are exact enough for practical purposes, and a lot better than if all that one man could say to another of a new apple was something like, "It's very interesting."

The two big classifications are "sweet" and "sour." Although nobody has felt any need to invent substitutes for "sweet," alternatives for "sour" are "subacid," "sprightly," and "tart." Any of these basic words can be accompanied by the qualifying words "mildly" or "very," when needed.

If a fruit has some astringency, the term "austere" is understood to indicate this.

The aromas of fruits are described in many ways, but two of the commonest basic terms are "rich," and "refreshing."

A fruit's flesh is described as to color, texture (firm, coarse, medium, fine; crisp, tender, tough), and juiciness (dry, juicy).

A fruit's *quality* means its combination of texture, flavor, and aroma, and is rated on a 6-point scale. Reading from the top, we have: best, very good, good, fair, poor, and very poor. There are very few fruits that rate "best," but also, luckily, few that rate "very poor," and even some of those are suffering more by comparison than by their integral quality.

APPLES

Everybody loves an apple and everybody always has —so much so that the apple is one of our most often used symbols, as in the expression, "the apple of his eye," for a favorite.

The apple is such an old fruit, it goes back beyond recorded history. There have been so many different known varieties of apples, thousands of them have disappeared without a trace. Some students of the subject, noting the existence of wild forests of apples in the Himalayas, believe this is the original home of the apple. Prehistoric man quickly realized the value of this fruit, to his credit, and began growing his own apple trees.

Whether or not this was the case with the ancient lake dwellers of Switzerland, we know they ate apples, because apples have been found, carbonized but recognizable, in the mud of the lake bottoms.

But although the apple has been with us all these millenia, unlike a few other very old fruits the traits of any variety of apple are not fixed in that variety's seeds, so that new varieties constantly occur when any seeds are planted. It is in this way, most often without any help from man, that good new varieties have come into the world.

Climate

There are few parts of the United States in which some kinds of apples will not grow, which is one reason apples are so immensely popular as a home-garden fruit. But if you live in Florida you'll have trouble finding an apple that will grow there, and the same is true if you live anywhere along the Gulf of Mexico or in Southern California. The difficulty in these climates is chiefly the lack of a winter cold enough to break the dormancy that an apple tree goes into, like a hibernating bear, after summer ends. For these climates a home gardener's best bet is a locally-obtained apple variety that has done well there. There are a few of these, and though fruit quality will not be equal to the best apples, any apple is a good apple if that's all you have. As we have said, Winter Banana is one such warm-climate variety. Miller carries it in semi-dwarf size (12 to 15 feet) on EM 7 rootstocks.

Pruning

Prune your dwarf apple tree in the cone shape. This will give you a sturdy tree whose higher branches don't shade those under them too much. Most apple trees bear their fruits on the short, gnarled twigs called spurs, and the spurs last for years; as a spur grows old it becomes more and more gnarled from sending out new buds in different directions each year. After your trees are six to eight years old you can prune off about one tenth of the oldest (most gnarled) spurs each winter.

Pollination

Apple blossoms need pollen from blossoms of another variety of apple before they can make fruit. Therefore, plant two trees of different kinds of apples to make sure of cross-pollination. There are a few, but only a few, varieties whose pollen is of no use, nearly always because they don't produce enough of it. Baldwin is one such, and others are Gravenstein, Mutsu, Rhode Island Greening, Spigold, and Winesap. If you grow one of these, plant *two* other varieties with it. As with the other fruits, bees will take care of the transfer of pollen from blossom to blossom, and unless the blossoming season is wet, overcast, cold, and generally miserable bee flying weather, the pollinating will get done.

Harvesting

The best eating apple is the one picked off the tree at

its peak of ripeness or soon after, before it begins to lose crispness. The best test is the simplest—taste one of the apples. If it is too sour, give the others more time to ripen. A ripe apple has a waxy skin and is well colored for its variety. If you are picking apples to store them, pick them *before* they are completely ripe, and store them in a cool room or basement. The technique of picking an apple is to grasp it and lift; it will come away clean if it is ripe enough.

Pests

The more common pests of apples are aphids, apple maggots, apple scab, borers, codling moths, curculio beetles, fire blight, leaf rollers, mites, and scale.

See Chapter 3 for descriptions and controls of each, Chapter 10 for sources and for further information on controls.

Varieties

Baldwin

Fifty years ago this big red apple, sometimes called Woodpecker apple, was the leader among all apples grown in the North and East, and a single standard-sized tree might shower down 20 barrels of the tough-skinned fruits. Today old Baldwin is hardly heard of, shouldered aside by Delicious, McIntosh, and others. And, though Baldwin was not as hardy a tree as some, and the fruit was never a true connoisseur's apple, it was and is a good eating apple—solid, crisp, juicy—and it holds a firm spot in the childhood memories of many older Americans today. Baldwin will pollinate neither itself nor other apples. (Leuthardt and Southmeadow)

Beacon

Starting in August, this attractive red apple ripens its fruits in succession for about a month, an excellent habit for a home garden fruit. Beacon is regarded fondly by many fanciers of apple quality, and is also a hardy apple, having originated in Minnesota. It can take Zone 3 weather with lows of -30° F. to -40° F. As you'd expect, it is a good keeper, too. (Farmer and Interstate)

Blue Pearmain

Like many of the handsomest apples, this one that gained its forename because of a grape-like bluish bloom on its skin cannot be called a superb eating apple, although it has good flavor, aromatic and sweet. The variety has not died out during the past 100-plus years, however, and one reason may be the hardiness of the trees. If you live where winters are unusually rugged, this old New England apple may be a good choice. Fruits ripen early in October. (Southmeadow)

Chieftain

This bright red apple is one of the many crosses that have been made of Red Delicious and Jonathan. This one was made during World War I at the Iowa Experiment Station, but was only recently introduced after years of testing. The flavor is between Jonathan's sprightliness and the rather bland sweetness of Delicious. Resistant to fire blight and scab, Chieftain is also a hardy variety, at home in Zone 4. (Field and Interstate)

Cortland

In 1898 the New York Agricultural Experiment Station breeders crossed a McIntosh with the tasteless old

Ben Davis that people used to say was like eating cotton, and the result was Cortland, an apple even better than the splendid McIntosh. The triumph goes to show what can be done if you have hope, and try anything. Sometimes called a salad apple because its white flesh stays white for a good while when cut, Cortland is an important apple in the Northeast, where it is grown commercially. (Kelly, Leuthardt, Mellinger, and N.Y. Co-op)

Dixie Red Delight

A red dessert apple that has a good reputation for regular bearing, this variety can get along with less winter chilling than most, and is a candidate for Zones 7 and 8, and for cooler parts of 9. Crops are large and the apples are well-distributed throughout the tree. Dixie is a particularly attractive tree in bloom. The variety is offered as a stempiece dwarf by Hastings.

Golden Delicious

This superb apple first saw the light of day when an apple seed sprouted on a farm hillside in West Virginia early in this century, and the owner let the tree grow along until he could see if the fruit was going to be worth keeping. Indeed it was, and when Paul Stark, Sr., of Stark Bro's Nurseries tasted it in 1914 he knew he had found something spectacular. A superb eating apple with a rich and aromatic flavor and agreeable tartness, Golden is also a fine cooking apple, an annual bearer, and an excellent pollinator for other varieties. Doing best in Zones 5 to 8, it ripens in October except in warmer California climates, where it ripens in summer. Stark lists a spur-type Golden (double-dwarf) which they say is especially disease-resistant, and nearly every other nursery carries Golden, usually on EM 9 roots.

Granny Smith

If you'd like to find out what the Australians consider a fine apple, grow Granny Smith. Seldom seen in American markets, Granny is top apple in Australia. Its skin is grass-green and shiny, the firm, crisp flesh is good for eating and cooking too, and the apples are splendid keepers. Granny ripens in November in the upper Midwest. (Southmeadow)

Gravenstein

This is one of the few Danish apples you can get, and when well grown it is such a good apple that even the critical English fruit connoisseur Edward Bunyard, author of the delightful *Anatomy of Dessert*, which deals entirely with fruits, waxed poetic over it: ". . . so full of juice and scented with the very attar of apple." We suspect he was used to better Gravensteins than we have tasted—but we have not tasted any grown in climates like Gravenstein's native Denmark. It is also a good cooking apple, and is popular for applesauce. The fruits are middle-sized and red-striped, although there is a large red sport that Southmeadow carries. Gravenstein is for Zones 3 to 8. It will pollinate neither itself nor other apples. (Leuthardt and Southmeadow)

Grimes Golden

Thought to be the male parent of Golden Delicious, Grimes also originated in West Virginia, but did so a good hundred years before its possible offspring did, about 1800. Grimes is a good apple and deserves its long popularity. Tart and spicy, it is a large golden-yellow apple, best eaten soon after its September harvest, as it doesn't keep well. Though adapted for Zones 5 to 8, Grimes is somewhat choosy about the particular spot where it wants to grow, so baby it a little (Boatman, Burpee, Interstate, and Southmeadow)

Jonadel

Like Chieftain, this is another cross of Jonathan and Red Delicious by the Iowa Experiment Station. It also is resistant to fire blight. Flavor is much like Chieftain, and so is the general appearance, both of them resembling Jonathan in looks and partly in tartness, and both being hardy to Zone 4. (Field)

Jonathan

If we had no apple except Jonathan we would still feel blessed. This sprightly apple has been so liked it has been crossed with many other varieties to produce several outstanding new kinds. Jonathan was itself a natural seedling, crossed by nature, and sprouted on a farm in New York state. A willing bearer, Jonathan is a cooking as well as a fine dessert apple. It is widely available at nurseries.

Jon-A-Red

This is another result of a cross between Jonathan and Red Delicious. It is exclusive with Stark, officially carrying the nursery name in front of its own. It is very good, and is especially at home in the Midwest.

Jumbo

Like Jon-A-Red, this is also a variety exclusive with Stark, which have long featured exclusives. Jumbo is chiefly notable for the size of its fruits, which run to about two pounds each, rivaling grapefruit in bulk, and looking like immense Red Delicious apples but tasting more of a Winesap tartness. Jumbo is one of those apples that originated not as a seedling but as a bud sport—a mutation on an existing tree, one limb bearing fruits in some way different than the others on the tree.

Lodi

Introduced in 1924 by the New York state experiment station, Lodi is a cross of Montgomery and Yellow Transparent. Lodi is an August apple in most areas, and is for Zones 4 to 8. It is resistant to fire blight, and for an early apple its quality is very good, especially when fruits are tree-ripened. Skin color is a bright yellow, dotted with brown, and flesh is white. Be especially alert to thinning here, as Lodi will skip every other year if you allow it to ripen too many fruits. (Burgess, Farmer, Field, Interstate, Kelly, Southmeadow, and Stark)

Macoun

This apple, like a few others such as Golden Delicious, is both a good market apple and also a good home garden one. Again like Golden Delicious, it is a good pollinator. The New York state experiment station bred Macoun in 1923 by crossing a McIntosh with a Jersey Black, and now considers Macoun the highest quality dessert apple grown in the Northeast. Macoun ripens in late September, has a handsome dark, striped skin, and crisp white, McIntosh-like flesh. (Kelly, Leuthardt, N.Y. Coop, and Southmeadow)

McIntosh

This excellent old apple originated in Canada about 200 years ago, apparently as a seedling of the old French apple, Fameuse, and like Fameuse its flesh is snow white. Skin color is red-striped, and eating quality of this apple is very good. Though somewhat prone to diseases, McIntosh has always been a popular tree with home gardeners in New England and New York. Two sub-varieties of McIntosh are offered more frequently now than the original—Red McIntosh and Early McIntosh. Early is a cross of McIntosh and Yellow Transparent, and ripens in August, about six weeks ahead of McIntosh. Most nurseries carry some kind of McIntosh, and Zones 3 to 5 are the best growing areas for them.

Mutsu

Bred in Japan, this big round yellow apple is a cross of Golden Delicious and Indo. It was introduced in 1948 and has been called the most promising new variety introduced at England's National Fruit Trials. Mutsu ripens in late October or even early November. Its dessert quality is quite high, juicy and crisp with a slightly spicy taste, and it is a splendid keeper, not shriveling in storage as its Golden Delicious parent may do. Mutsu should have two different apple varieties as companion trees, since it can neither pollinate itself nor others. (N.Y. Co-op, and Southmeadow)

Northern Spy

This remarkably fine apple is still seen in some markets but they grow fewer by the year, so if you want to be sure you can taste one of the best late apples ever bred, grow Northern Spy for yourself. The fruit is beautifully red, the white flesh is crisp and juicy, the quality so fine that U. P. Hedrick, the American fruit authority, rated it "very good to best." The tree blooms late and thereby escapes some spring frosts that kill blossoms of others.

Northern Spy grew from a seed planted by an experimenter in New Jersey about 1800, and became a great favorite, despite its deplorable habit of taking 10 years or more to start bearing. As a dwarf tree, though, this time is cut to about four years—not speedy, but well worth the wait. Northern Spy ripens in November. Zones 4 to 6.

(Ackerman, Kelly, Leuthardt, Mellinger, and South-meadow)

Red Delicious

The original Delicious apple grew from a seed, on an Iowa farm in 1872, probably a cross of Winesap and Yellow Bellflower. It was introduced by Stark Bro's in 1893, and became so popular with commercial growers that for years it has been the leading market apple in the U.S. and one of the most important in the world.

Double-Red Delicious, or Starking, is a bud sport and is identical except for coloring earlier and looking more luscious. Both carry the familiar five knobs on the bottom, and both are so-called sweet apples, not tart. They ripen in September in most regions, and are for Zones 5 to 8. They are carried by most nurseries, and Stark has several kinds.

Rhode Island Greening

Although this old Colonial variety refused to grow in very northern or southern parts of the country, and had some other faults, it was so good a dessert and cooking apple that it swept all others aside and became America's favorite green apple (actually, yellowish-green). After 250 years it is still popular, its flavor rich, refreshing, tart. And it is still a good home-garden apple, as it has always been, ripening in late October. It will pollinate neither itself nor other apples. (Leuthardt and Southmeadow)

Rome Beauty

This is an old apple from Ohio, an excellent baking apple and also good fresh. Though the trees are apt to be shorter-lived than most, they bear well, and a fault of failing to turn satisfactorily red was corrected when some red sports were discovered. Rome ripens in October and is for Zones 5 to 8. (Boatman and Waynesboro)

Spigold

This big, red-striped apple came from the New York state experiment station in 1962, and is so good that it can be forgiven the fact that it is not a worthwhile pollinator. Plant it with two other varieties. It is a cross of Red Spy and Golden Delicious, and its fine-grained yellow flesh is so delectable, sprightly yet sweet, that it ranks with the best of apples that are its seniors by centuries. It ripens in October. Zones appear to be 4 to 6 or 7. (N.Y. Co-op, and Southmeadow)

Starkspur Earli Blaze

This good big red summer apple with a sprightly flavor is a heavy bearer and fair keeper. Especially important, the trees are resistant to scab, mildew, and blotch. The fruit should be thinned to 8 inches apart to keep trees bearing annually. Ripening is in August. Zones 5 to 8. (Stark)

Stayman Winesap

This well-known dessert apple was raised in Kansas from a seed of a Winesap in the 1860s and was named for the man who planted the seed, Dr. J. Stayman. Like Winesap, it is a very good dessert apple. Most of the Staymans offered by nurseries are red sports. Harvest time is late October. Zones 5 to 7. (Boatman, Burpee, Hastings, Mellinger, Southmeadow, and Waynesboro)

Wealthy

Originating in St. Paul, but from a seed that came from New England, this good red apple has red-tinted white flesh that earned it a deserved reputation for quality. It is both a cooking and fresh-eating apple. Ripening in September, it is a particularly good tree in colder areas, but will do well from Zones 3 to about 6. (Farmer, Gurney, Interstate, Leuthardt, Mellinger, and Southmeadow)

Winesap

What we said of Stayman Winesap applies generally to this apple, its maternal parent. An old apple, excellent keeper, and thought to have been originally called Wine Sop, it makes excellent cider, which is unusual for a good dessert apple. Ripening in late October, it is for Zones 5 to 7. It will pollinate neither itself nor other apples. (Field, Gurney, Interstate, Leuthardt, Savage, and Waynesboro)

Yellow Transparent

A hardy apple, doing especially well in colder regions, Yellow Transparent like its offspring Lodi is a summer apple, bright yellow, tart, and good. (Ackerman, Boatman, Southmeadow, and Waynesboro)

PEARS

People have been singing the praises of pears for heaven knows how long—ever since mankind stopped living on the hunting trail and settled down to gardening. In trying to describe the texture of this luscious fruit, "buttery" is the word that keeps popping up. One of the good ways to enjoy a choice, dead-ripe pear is to spoon out its buttery flesh, savoring it at leisure on the half-shell, you might say.

As with apples, though not as much so, you have a wide choice of varieties with pears if you live in pear country, the best regions being north of Zone 7 in the

East and Midwest, and the West Coast states.

The ancients knew and loved the pear, and cultivated several varieties; the Romans had 40 or more. It is thought that the original home of the pear was the Caucasian countries, and as with the apple, forests of pears were found growing wild in the Himalayan Mountains. Also like the apple, pear trees are long-lived; some have lived for an amazing 400 years, and 75 years can be regarded as a normal life expectancy for a pear tree.

Early colonists brought the pear to America, and in fact the pear outranked the apple in America's youth as the pet of gentlemen fruit gardeners and of the great nineteenth-century pomologists, when hundreds of new varieties were introduced.

The pioneer American farmers greatly valued the pear even though they couldn't store pears for months, like apples. But they could store the juice of pears, called "perry," and pear wood was much coveted for making furniture and tool handles. They also steeped pear leaves to make a yellow dye.

Climate

If your climate will suit an apple tree it will probably suit a pear tree, and in fact a few varieties of pears will fruit in the far-south and far-north zones where apples generally will not. This tolerance will not do home gardeners much good at present, since only one of the varieties that thrive in the extreme climates is available in dwarf form (Kieffer; see Chapter 8); if any others are available, we haven't run across any suppliers. Our best suggestion is that you inquire at your local nurseries.

An overly-rich soil is apt to make pear trees such lush growers that they are easily hurt by fire blight—so do not feed them richly, either.

Pears need some winter cold to end dormancy; the

amount of cold (in hours) depends on the variety. Late spring frosts don't usually harm fruit set, as pears are not early bloomers.

Pruning

Grow pears as you do apples, in cone shape. Only a little annual pruning is needed, and the main point to watch is to keep the trees from growing *too* cone-shaped. The cure is to prune back some of the most upright limbs, cutting just above an outward-pointing leaf bud. Wood that grows upward instead of outward seldom bears much fruit.

Pollination

Nearly all pear trees depend on other pear trees to pollinate their blossoms. Fortunately, most pear trees *will* pollinate others. An exception among those we list below is Magness. Two others, Bartlett and Seckel, can pollinate other pears but can't pollinate each other. Duchess, bless her, will set fruit without being cross-pollinated, and will pollinate any other pear, too.

Harvesting

The pear that ripens perfectly on the tree is rare. The thing to do is to pick pears before they are ripe, when they are still quite firm and hard, then bring them inside, wrap them in soft paper, and put them in a cool but draft-free room to ripen.

It is usually time to start picking when the first few fruits drop. At this time, the more advanced pears will be changing to a yellowish color, and if you take hold of a pear and lift it, it will come off the stem if it is ready to be picked. Take the most nearly ripe ones each day until the crop is all picked and stored.

How long must a pear be stored before it is ready to eat? This is quite iffy, taking from a day or two to several weeks. Early pears usually ripen fastest, winter pears slowest. When they *do* ripen, store them in plastic bags in the refrigerator to keep them at their perfection.

Pests

The same insects that attack apple trees may attack pears, though not generally as seriously. Those to watch out for include borers, codling moths, fire blight, mites, pear psylla, scab, and scale.

See Chapter 3 for descriptions and controls, and Chapter 10 for sources of and further information on controls.

Varieties

Anjou

This old pear from France matures in August or September in the Midwest, but as late as October in some climates. It has had a good reputation with pear fanciers for years and years, partly because it is so willing a keeper and thus extends the pear season. Also known as Beurre d'Anjou, it is a big yellowish-green pear with sprightly white flesh. It is most at home in Zones 5 to 7. (Leuthardt, Miller, and Stark)

Bartlett

Certainly the most widely known pear, Bartlett is also one of the older varieties—about 200 years old. It originated in England from a seed, and was first named Williams. Despite some put-downs from pear gourmets, Bartlett pleases most people immensely. It is a rich yellow with a reddish blush, has buttery flesh that is just tart enough, and is a good cooking pear as well as being good for eating fresh. It ripens in August or September, and does best in Zones 5 to 7. Practically every nursery carries a dwarf Bartlett.

Beurre Bosc

Dr. Van Mons of Belgium raised this famous pear from a seed in 1807 and it became one of the world's best. It is a long-necked pear, yellow with light brown blotching. The buttery flesh is juicy, piquant, and aromatic, ranking at the top of the pear list alongside Seckel. Fruits ripen in October. (Leuthardt, Southmeadow, and Stark)

Clapp Favorite

Considered a good home-garden pear, Clapp is much like Bartlett in looks, and is a sweet, fine-grained fruit to eat and to cook. Ripening time is late August or early September. This variety has a reputation for hardiness. Zones 5 to 7. (Ackerman, Burgess, Burpee, Kelly, Leuthardt, Miller, and Southmeadow)

Colette

This is a new pear that looks much like a Bartlett and is a good eating and cooking pear. It will never be a commercial variety, for a reason that recommends it to the home gardener—a habit of maturing its fruits over a span of six or eight weeks. The first pears are ready for picking in late August, and others continue to ripen until frost ends the season. Zones 5 to 7. (Miller)

Duchess

This excellent old pear, also called Duchesse d'Angouleme or just Angouleme, bears yellowish-green fruits that may weigh 20 ounces each. They start maturing in September in the Midwest, and in October in the Northeast. They keep well and are delicious—juicy, buttery, lightly spicy. Best of all, Duchess is self-fruitful so that it can set fruit when planted alone and will also act as a pollinator for any other pear. Zones 5 to 7. (Field, Interstate, Kelly, Leuthardt, Mellinger, and Stark)

Gorham

The New York state experiment station bred this good pear by crossing Bartlett with a delicious old European pear called Josephine deMalines, and introduced the offspring in 1923. It looks much like Bartlett, and ripens about two weeks later, in latter September. However, Gorham is a better keeper, holding for about two months in cold storage—which can be an old refrigerator for a home gardener. The New York station notes that Gorham trees need a little extra nitrogen, so give them up to 20 percent more blood meal than other pears in the spring fertilizing. Zones 5 to 7. (N.Y. Co-op and Southmeadow)

Maxine

Resistance to fire blight is the outstanding quality of this pear, although it has also been praised by some for its large size, bright yellow color, and fine flavor. Maxine is a late summer ripener in the Midwest. Zones 5 to 7. (Interstate, Miller, and Southmeadow)

Magness

Another blight-resistant variety, Magness is a U.S. Department of Agriculture development. It is a mid-September pear in the Midwest, and an excellent keeper, lasting until nearly Christmas in cold storage. Fruits are of a good size and of high quality. The variety's main drawback is an inability to produce pollen for cross-pollination, so plant two other varieties (or just Duchess) with Magness. Zones 5 to 7. (Ackerman, Southmeadow, and Stark)

Seckel

Often considered the standard of excellence among

pears, Seckel isn't much to look at—small and brownish
—but its honeyed spiciness sends pear lovers into ec-
stasies. A good deal of the flavor is in the skin, which is
tender and good. Seckel is a self-made pear, originating
on its own as a seedling on a Pennsylvania farm about
200 years ago. It is resistant to fire blight and is a good
producer. Seckel will ripen on the tree in September, or
can be ripened on the shelf as are other pears. The trees
do best in richer soil than other pears want. Zones 5 to 7
and northern parts of 8. (Burpee, Gurney, Interstate,
Leuthardt, Mellinger, Miller, Southmeadow, Stark, and
Waynesboro)

Starkrimson

This is a bright red Clapp Favorite, having originated
as a bud sport on a Clapp tree. In other respects it is just
like Clapp. Zones 5 to 7. (Stark)

Tyson

An old American pear and a good one, Tyson is nevertheless hard to find today. It ripens in August, is blight-
resistant and hardy. Fruits are medium-sized, attractively yellow, and so good that Tyson is also called Summer
Seckel. Tyson fruits can be allowed to ripen on the tree.
Incidentally, this is an especially good variety for training
as an espalier, explained in Chapter 6. Zones 5 to 8.
(Stark)

PEACHES

Sometimes the liberties taken with a word hint at how
people regard the real thing the word stands for, and
"peach," when it doesn't refer to the fruit, always refers
to something much prized. Good reason, too, for peaches
are luscious. The word, incidentally, derives from the
word "Persia," but the peach is native to eastern Asia,

and the Chinese were growing peaches 3000 years ago. Early sixteenth-century settlers brought the peach to America, where it absolutely flourished.

In fact, although the peach cannot take the rough weather and neglect that the apple may cheerfully live through, the peach is nonetheless scattered all over the world, changing its looks and to some extent its habits according to where it finds itself. Thus, there have been peaches that store nearly as well as apples, peaches that weigh a pound, peaches that bear fruit on spurs along their trunks like spur-type apple trees, and so on.

Surprisingly for so adaptable a fruit, the peach is far more stable genetically when grown from seed than are apples or pears. If you plant a peach seed you stand a good chance of growing a worthwhile crop even though the variety will not be exactly the same as the parent, or may be a nectarine.

Climate

By and large, peaches don't produce fruit if winter temperatures drop below 15° F., but there are some hardy exceptions, noted in the variety list that follows, and in Chapter 8. But though sensitive to excessive cold, the peach needs some winter cold to break its dormancy. All peaches grow in the broad middle belt that comprises Zones 5 to 8, with a few varieties doing well north or south of that belt. It is a fact, though, that *some* kind of peach will grow in every state of the continental U.S.

Pruning

Prune your peach tree in the vase shape. The peach grows new wood at a great rate, which is good as it depends on new wood to produce each year's crop. Look at a peach shoot at the end of the summer and you'll find the farthest-out growth (two or three feet long) is glossy and reddish and has leaves, not fruit. But it will have fruit the next year—and a good deal too much unless you prune off a third or more of the shoot. Even so, you'll have to thin the fruits that do form.

Additional pruning consists of cutting older shoots out entirely, to let sunlight into the trees, and cutting back any too-upright shoots to an outward-pointing bud.

In the case of genetic dwarf peaches, growth is much less rambunctious, so that little pruning is needed.

Pollination

Most peaches will set fruit without another peach tree nearby, and this is the case with all those we list below.

Harvesting

Peaches should be allowed to *almost* ripen on the tree, and this is the kind of peach you must grow for yourself if you are to find out how delectable this queen of summer fruits can be. To tell when to pick a peach, grasp it gently and twist it slightly. It will come free if ready. Then put it gently in a comfortable room temperature, in the 70s, and it will be ready the next day. Store it in the refrigerator at that time if you aren't ready to eat it at once.

Pests

Aphids, borers, brown rot, curculio beetles, leaf-curl, mites, Oriental fruit moths, and scale may trouble the peach.

See Chapter 3 for descriptions and controls, and Chapter 10 for sources or further information on controls.

Varieties

Bonanza

This beautiful little tree with its luxuriant foliage

thickly placed on the branches is as much an ornamental as a working fruit tree. It is the first genetic dwarf that was also worth growing for its peaches as a fresh dessert fruit. Armstrong Nurseries did the breeding, working with Swatow peach, a naturally dwarfed species from China. Bonanza starts bearing its big red-blushed freestone fruits when it is still just a little thing no higher than your waistline, and it stays small, growing to about 6 feet when mature, though you can keep it lower than that, to 4 or 5 feet, with top pruning. Ripening is in August. Zones 5 to 8. (Armstrong, Burpee, Field, and Kelly)

EarliGlo

This is an early peach, ripening in the Midwest in mid-July. It is yellow-fleshed and freestone, and so productive that heavy thinning—to 8 inches between the small green fruits—is needed to produce full-sized, 3-inch-wide fruits. Quality is good for so early a peach, and the trees have a good reputation for hardiness. Zones 5 to 8. (Stark)

Elberta

Now about 100 years old, Elberta is still the best known peach in America. Though excelling as a market peach, we include it here because it is so dependable. And though epicures seldom include Elberta among choice varieties, a home-grown Elberta is in our opinion nothing to look down on—tender, juicy, and delightful. As probably everyone knows, Elberta is a yellow-skinned peach with a lovely red blush, yellow-fleshed and freestone. It ripens in late August, does best in Zones 5 to 8, and practically every nursery lists it.

Golden Jubilee

Hardy enough to take a New England winter, this big

yellow freestone peach is a development of the New Jersey experiment station. It is a regular producer and has the happy habit of blooming late enough to escape most frosts. Juicy and sweet, it ripens its tender-skinned fruits in later August. Zones 5 to 8. (Burpee, Kelly, Leuthardt, Mellinger, Miller, and Savage)

Hale Haven

One of the newer peaches, this is a very good fresh dessert fruit and is also one of the best peaches for canning. The large deep-yellow fruits are freestone, and the skin is tough enough to make this a shipping peach— though this is no drawback for a home gardener. Trees are good producers, and fruits ripen in late August or early September. Zones 5 to 8. (Ackerman, Boatman, Burpee, Field, Hastings, Interstate, Leuthardt, and Miller).

July Elberta

Ripening about a month before Elberta, this peach can be considered a superior Elberta in quality and just as dependable a producer as Elberta. It was named by the Stark Nurseries, but is not related to Elberta so far as is known, being a peach Luther Burbank was working with at the time of his death in 1926. Burbank's method was to make so many crosses in the course of an experiment that there is now no telling what the parentage of July Elberta was. Zones 5 to 8 and cooler parts of 9. (Stark)

Polly

This is a very good white-fleshed peach that is also hardier than white-fleshed peaches are apt to be. Polly can take -15° F. The large white-skinned fruits blushed with red ripen in August and are freestone, with juicy, sprightly flesh. Zones 6 to 8 and warmer parts of Zone 5. (Field, Gurney, and Interstate)

Redhaven

This development from Michigan State University (as you can tell from the "haven" in the name, always found on Michigan State's peaches) is, like Elberta, popular with both commercial and home fruit growers. It is rapidly becoming the standard early peach according to the New York State Fruit Testing Cooperative Association. Redhaven is a yellow-fleshed freestone ripening in August or late July. Because the fruit doesn't turn brown quickly when cut, it is popular for freezing. As with EarliGlo, the fruits should be thinned severely and early as the trees are very productive. They are also able to take a good deal of cold weather. Nearly every mail order nursery carries a dwarf Redhaven, and Stark have a mutation they call Compact Redhaven that they compare with their excellent double-dwarf apples in size and performance. Zones 5 to 8.

Starking Delicious

Fairly new, this big red peach with yellow flesh arose when one branch on a tree of the excellent July Elberta ripened its peaches early. Quality is virtually identical with July Elberta. Starking Delicious ripens early enough —mid-July—to make it of special interest. It is freestone when tree-ripe, and should be thinned hard, to 8 inches between young fruits. Zones 5 to 8 and cooler parts of 9. (Stark)

Starlet

This pretty little thing is a genetic dwarf, sister or at least kissing cousin, to Bonanza. The rich yellow fruits blushed with bright red are freestone and yellow-fleshed, good quality, and the trees are as ornamental as Bonanza

and as at home in an ornamental planting or a container
as they are in the fruit garden. Zones 5 to 8. (Stark)

NECTARINES

Arguments still break out about whether nectarines
and peaches are the same species, but botanists are practically unanimous in the opinion that the two trees are
identical, their flower and leaf physiology is identical,
and the two fruits share the same characters in colors of
flesh, and in being freestone or clingstone. True, nectarines are fuzzless, their flesh is generally firmer, more aromatic, and usually juicier than that of peaches. But, say
the experts, they are the same, for all of that, and so
share the same botanical name, *Prunus persica.* As a
clinching argument, plant a peach seed and you may
very well grow a nectarine tree. And a nectarine seed may
sprout into a peach tree.

Another fallacy we sometimes run across is the idea
that the peach is old, the nectarine new. Not a bit of it.
Nectarines were delighting the human palate so long ago
that Julius Caesar may have eaten them.

Good new nectarines have been developed in recent
years, including genetic dwarfs, and it is interesting to
notice that the close relationship of peaches and nectarines is actually a complication in a breeding program.
Here is how a world authority on fruit, and research head
of pioneering Stark Bro's Nurseries, Paul Stark, Jr., explained it in the *American Fruit Grower,* leading U.S.
trade publication in its field:

"All of the new nectarines originally came to us as
mutations of peaches, but the new and better varieties
have peach blood in the crosses, to get large size and
firmness. When peaches are brought into the breeding,
however, all the first-generation progeny come as
peaches, and it is necessary to back-cross to get the one
out of four nectarines in true Mendellian recessive segre-

gation. [The 25 percent of every second-generation off-spring that will continue to breed true to a recessive character—in this case to bearing nectarine fruits rather than peach fruits.]That is why the route to nectarine improvement has been much longer than peach improvement and has also involved many more crosses."

What has been said of peaches as to climate, pruning, pollination, harvesting, and pests, applies also to nectarines.

Varieties

Note: Most nurseries carry some kind of dwarf nectarine. The nurseries mentioned here specify the varieties they carry.

Hunter

The large fruits are semi-freestone and are juicy, tender, and of very good quality. Zones 5 to 8. (Leuthardt)

Morton

A development of the New York experiment station, this new semi-clingstone nectarine ripens early—in August—and although not a large fruit, it is juicy and very good. Skin color is dark red, the flesh greenish. But the point to note most particularly about Morton is its resistance to brown rot—a big plus in any home-garden planting. Zones 5 to 8. (N.Y. Co-op and Southmeadow)

Nectacrest

Introduced by the New Jersey experiment station in 1947, this big white-fleshed nectarine is freestone and of high quality. Skin is bright red, shading to pink, and fruits ripen in early September. The trees are hardy and are strong growers. Zones 6 to 8 and milder parts of 5. (Miller)

Nectarina

This, along with Bonanza peach, is a genetic dwarf and is also a development bred at the Armstrong Nurseries. The growth habit of the trees is as compact as Bonanza, and they are equally as decorative. Fruit skin color is a rich red on a yellow ground, and the juicy flesh is orange-colored, firm, and good. Zones 5 to 8. (Armstrong and Burpee)

SunGlo

An unusually large nectarine, some fruits weighing a pound, this is a vigorous new variety developed by one of the most successful modern plant breeders, Fred Anderson, Merced, California. Although the Anderson developments have generally been aimed at commercial growers, this nectarine is a good one for home gardeners to consider. Quality of the big red freestone fruits is excellent, and the trees are exceptionally winter-hardy (a trait that was not formerly associated with nectarines). Fruits start ripening in early August in the Midwest. Thin the young fruits early to get the size of mature fruits this tree can give you. Zones 5 to 8. (Stark)

PLUMS

The two types of plums you can buy at the market for eating are European and Japanese, and you will be offered only those varieties that can take the rigors of travel and storage, of course. These market plums at the best are good, but you can grow some in your garden a great deal better, letting them ripen on the trees instead of having to pick them green to ship well, and by planting some you will never find offered as fresh fruit at all.

In addition to European and Japanese plums, there are Damson plums (also from Europe, but mostly used for jam and preserves), and American plums; the American ones are native to this country, and the one you are most apt to find offered as a dwarf is the Beach plum, *Prunus maritima*, which is dwarf by habit. Its small purple fruits have sour skins and sweet flesh and are more cooking plums than fresh-eating ones, but they are willing to grow in some places where the better sorts will not. We cover them in Chapter 8.

European plums include the sweetest varieties, and their flesh is usually firm. Their predominant skin color is blue, though there are greenish, yellowish, and reddish European plums. All prunes are really European plums of varieties that are extra sweet, for only a very sweet plum can be dried successfully without removing the seed. The European plum is an old fruit, probably originating in the region of the Caucasus Mountains, where warlike nomads such as the Huns and Mongols gathered them for fresh food and for drying.

Damson plums are usually seen in their blue or purple forms, but there are yellow Damsons too. The Damson is an old plum like the European plum. Damsons will come true from seed, but planting one of the suckers that spring up from the roots is a faster way to get fruit. In neither case, however, will you get a *dwarf* tree, although a standard Damson is by nature fairly small. There are some sweet Damsons, but as we said, Damsons are regarded as cooking plums, and reach their triumph as preserves.

Japanese plums originated in China. Reds and orange-reds predominate among the Japanese plums, with some greenish or yellowish coloring here and there. These plums are generally softer and juicier than European ones, and are less sweet, but as dessert fruits they are beautiful and delicious.

Climate

In America, European plums do not grow well or sometimes at all in the South and Southwest, and do best on the East and West Coasts and the Great Lakes region. A rule of thumb is, if you can grow most varieties of pears where you live, you can plant European plums with fair assurance they will do well.

Damsons are much less finicky about where they will grow, and can take colder winters.

Except for the coldest areas, Japanese plums will grow where European plums will, and also can be raised in some southern and southwestern areas where European plums won't do well. If peaches do well for you, you can try Japanese plums.

In dry spells young plum trees may need watering, as well as the mulching that all fruit trees should have. If you live in dry country and need to irrigate, plums will need it during their blossoming and fruiting periods.

Pruning

Plums of every type bear their fruits on spurs, but since Japanese plums bear fruit more heavily than the others, they can stand more pruning.

Prune dwarf *European* and *Damson* plums in cone shape, as you do dwarf apple trees, and keep the spurs producing fruit. Remove too-vertical branches, or if you can't spare them, an alternative to removal is to pull them down to a more horizontal position, as explained in Chapter 8.

In pruning lateral branches, take it easy and don't prune away any of them unless they are poorly placed. The reason is, the fruit spurs are on these branches and it is possible to overprune these trees to the point where you will have cut off most of the fruiting wood. Simply prune off about half the length of the longest laterals only, and remove enough branches to keep the trees open to sun.

This pruning will also take care of as much fruit thinning as these trees need.

Japanese plums are grown in the vase shape. Some varieties even grow a little too vase-shaped, and will need to have some lateral branches shortened, to encourage more upright growth. A few varieties, chiefly Santa Rosa in the listing below, like to grow more upright than necessary, however, and the cure for this is to cut back some upright branches to outward-pointing buds.

The Japanese plums have fruit spurs all through the trees, and there is no chance that you will cut off so many that you won't have any fruit. These trees are strong growers, too, and annual pruning is a matter of removing misplaced branches, watersprouts, and older wood. You'll also need to thin the fruits to 3 or 4 inches apart.

Pollination

Most Damsons are self-fruitful. Many European plums are also self-fruitful but all Europeans bear better crops if cross-pollinated with some other variety of European plum. Japanese plums need cross-pollination with another Japanese plum variety.

Harvesting

A ripe plum can be squeezed (lightly!), but a green one is hard to the touch. Give the ripe one a slight twist and it will come off the tree. The right harvesting stage is the dead-ripe one unless you want the tartness that almost-ripe plums have. Japanese plums can be picked at this almost-ripe stage and allowed to finish ripening in a cool room, if an early picking is more convenient for you. Even when dead-ripe, nearly all plums will keep for about a week in a cool room, and they don't need as careful handling as many fruits do. Fortunately for the home gardener, every last plum on the tree doesn't ripen on the same day, so the picking can go on at a comfortable pace for a week or so.

Pests

The most common plum pests are aphids, black knot, borers, brown rot, curculio beetles, scale, and yellow-leaf. Apple maggots may attack European plums.

See Chapter 3 for descriptions and controls, and Chapter 10 for further information on and suppliers of controls.

Varieties

Abundance

This Japanese plum has medium-sized red fruit, with juicy, clingstone, yellow flesh, ripening in August. Luther Burbank, known especially for his success with plums, developed the Abundance. Zones 5 to 9. (Boatman, Burpee, Leuthardt, and Waynesboro)

Burbank

This is a fine reddish Japanese plum with sweet yellow clingstone flesh. It is good both for eating fresh and for canning, and bears prolifically. Zones 5 to 9. (Burpee, Kelly, Leuthardt, Mellinger, Savage, and Waynesboro)

Damsons

You can eat a Damson plum fresh if you let it ripen thoroughly on the tree, which will be in September, but Damsons are best known for the rich and full-flavored preserves they make. There are several varieties but Shropshire or what is called Blue Damson will be what you usually find. The trees bear loads of their little plums, and most varieties are self-fruitful. You need not thin the fruit.

We have found Damson trees quite persistent about throwing up suckers around the base of their trunks. As mentioned, these can be transplanted but will grow into standard trees. However, even a standard Damson is a small tree, 10 to 12 feet tall. Dwarfs grow to 6 feet or a little more. Nearly every nursery carries a Damson, but the ones listed below carry a dwarf type; Damsons are adapted to Zones 5 to 9 and some milder parts of 4. (Boatman, Burgess, and Leuthardt)

Elephant Heart

This great big Japanese plum was one of Luther Burbank's triumphs. The greenish skin turns a ruddy purple to signal ripeness, at which time the deep red flesh is so soft and juicy it is almost liquid, and its flavor will remind you of a sweet cherry. A sandy soil suits Elephant Heart best, and it wants less feeding and watering than most plums. It does best in Zones 5 to 9, but can be difficult in the East, really preferring semi-arid parts of the West, and sandy areas in the Southeast. (Southmeadow)

German Prune

This is a very old variety. It ripens its fruit over a two-week period or so; they are of good quality, sweet as are all prunes, and a deep purple. Zones 5 to 7. (Leuthardt)

Green Gage

Also called Reine Claude and many other names (having been dubbed Green Gage by accident, but too long ago to change now), this old European plum is greenish-yellow and is a fine dessert fruit. It is also a favorite for cooking, and is freestone. Ripening is in mid-August. Zones 5 to 7. (Leuthardt and Southmeadow)

Howard Miracle

This is a Japanese plum, a new variety with which we are not familiar, but one said to be outstanding in flavor, its skin tenderness making it especially a home-garden plum. Also, the ripening period begins about mid-July and extends into August. Skin is apricot-colored, and fruits are large. Zones 6 to 9 and milder parts of 5. (Miller)

Italian Prune

A very good quality plum, sweet and juicy, this variety is also called Fellenburg. Skin is purple-black, the fruits medium-sized and freestone. The yellow flesh is quite tart despite its prune character; it is good as a fresh dessert and for cooking. Zones 5 to 7. (Leuthardt and Miller)

Santa Rosa

Of all Japanese plums this is the best known, the most widely grown commercial plum in California, but also a good variety for the home garden. As it ripens on the tree, Santa Rosa is a beautiful sight; it turns from a striking red to purplish when fully ripe. Tree-ripened, Santa Rosa is a fine dessert plum to eat fresh, its clingstone reddish-yellow flesh juicy and rich for a Japanese type. The plums keep fairly well, too. Zones 5 to 9. (Boatman, Kelly, Leuthardt, and Miller)

Stanley Prune

Introduced by the New York experiment station in 1926, this excellent prune has proven so vigorous, hardy, and productive, it is replacing the Italian Prune in the Northeast and is now the prune most widely listed by the big nurseries. The large, dark blue freestone fruits ripen in early September and should be let ripen fully on the tree to bring out their good quality—firmly fine-grained, tender, sweet, and juicy. Zones 5 to 7. (Ackerman, Boatman, Burpee, Field, Interstate, Kelly, Leuthardt, Mellinger, and Miller)

CHERRIES

Each year cherries lead the pretty parade of the fruits, blossoming early and ripening so quickly that, when we lived in the Midwest, we were picking our tartly delicious Montmorencies a month before summer had officially begun. If we were there now we would add to the planting a dwarf Windsor, a Schmidt's Bigarreau, and a Yellow Spanish, which would give us a nice combination of red and yellow sweet cherries, too, and would provide the cross-pollination sweet cherries need.

These two main groups of cherries, sour ones and sweet ones, account for most of the cherries grown. There is a third group of cherries, the Dukes. These are hybrids, the result of cross-breeding between sweet cherries and sour ones. Duke trees resemble sweet cherry trees, and Duke fruits look much like sour cherries. Some such crosses have been made by man in recent horticultural history, but most Duke cherries are old varieties and came about by chance. To be frank about it, though, nursery stock of Dukes are hard to find today, now that there are easier-to-grow sweet cherries and less sour sour cherries. As with many hybrid plants, Duke seeds are apt to be sterile, though you can grow a cherry tree, and often a good one, by planting the seed of a sweet cherry or a sour one. You'll get a standard, not a dwarf, in that case, even though the seed may be from a cherry on a dwarf tree.

Even standard sizes of sour cherry trees are small compared to sweet cherries. A standard sour cherry tree often stays under 20 feet, and our Montmorencies were no more than 12 feet tall, but 40 feet is not at all uncommon for a sweet cherry. Therefore, home gardeners can be happy that sweet cherries especially can be found in at least a few varieties as dwarfs—or more accurately, as semi-dwarfs, for they grow 10 to 12 feet tall.

Climate

Sweet cherries have a reputation for being difficult, refusing to do well where summers are very hot, disliking humidity, but demanding more winter cold than sour cherries to break their dormant period. There is something to all this, and if you live in northern Minnesota or southern Louisiana you'll be wasting time if you plant sweet cherries in your garden. But we have seen and heard of enough exceptions to the rules to lead us to say: If you think your home is in a borderline area, go ahead and try sweet cherries. If they succeed, look what you've gained.

Except for the coldest climates, you can plant cherries in the fall. They are the only fruit covered in this book that somewhat prefer fall planting where it is possible.

Sour cherries are more tolerant of cold weather than sweet ones, and most of them will grow as far north as Zone 4. Most sweet cherries do not thrive farther north than Zone 5, and may do poorly in less favored Zone 5 areas. Both sour and sweet cherries will grow as far south as Zone 7, but neither is very happy farther south, although a new natural dwarf sour cherry, North Star, will grow in some cooler parts of Zone 8.

Pruning

Dwarf cherry trees are pruned to the cone shape. Pay special attention to the tendency some sweet cherries have of throwing up vertical branches, which will reduce fruit production. Prune these branches back to a lateral twig or bud. Otherwise, pruning should be light, for the fruiting spurs last for several years. Merely keep the interior of the tree open to sunlight by removing crowding branches, and shorten any fruiting branches that grow too long.

Pollination

Sour cherries are self-fruitful. Sweet cherries need cross-pollination with another sweet cherry, either dwarf or standard.

Harvesting

Always let cherries ripen on the tree. And when you pick them, pick the stems too, for a better quality product. A ripe sour cherry will come free easily when you take hold of it. In a sweet cherry the mark of ripeness is a sudden firmness. Store surplus cherries in the refrigerator, where they will keep for a week or more.

Pests

Pests of cherry trees are aphids, apple maggots, birds, black knot, borers, brown rot, curculio beetles, mites, scale (mainly on sweet cherry trees), and yellow-leaf.

See Chapter 3 for descriptions and controls, Chapter 10 for sources of and further information on controls.

Varieties

Black Tartarian

As its name suggests, this is a Russian cherry, though it has been grown in America for more than 150 years. It is a fine black cherry, sweet and rich. Fruits are not immense, and are somewhat soft, which is characteristic of the so-called Heart cherries, making Tartarian more a home-garden cherry than some, although it is also shipped. The trees are not always good producers as they grow indifferently in certain areas, but they are well worth growing where they do well. The crop ripens in June. Zones 5 to 7. (Leuthardt)

Giant

This sweet cherry was a Luther Burbank fruit, a complex hybrid, dark red and good. Burbank named three cherries "Giant," and one, Black Giant, was probably the same as Giant. The third, Improved Giant, disappeared from sight and never seems to have reached the market, but Giant is a good late cherry, worth a home gardener's time—juicy, rich, and sweet. Zones 5 to 7. (Southmeadow)

Montmore

This can be considered a low-growing Montmorency, and what is said of Montmorency applies to Montmore. A low semi-dwarf, Montmore tops off at 12 feet or a little less. Fruits turn almost black when ripe, and crops are large. Zones 4 to cooler parts of 8. (Field)

Montmorency

Most popular of the sour cherries, and now available in dwarf form, this fine variety has yellow flesh that is not too tart to eat fresh if allowed to ripen on the tree. The big red cherries ripen in late May or June, blooming late enough to escape any but an unusually late frost. And if you have a great deal of wet weather during the fruiting season, Montmorency cherries will not crack open nearly so easily as most varieties. Control with pruning any tendency to grow too tall. Stark is carrying a spur-type mutation Montmorency that should get around this problem. Zones 4 to 7. (Interstate, Leuthardt, Savage, Southmeadow, and Stark)

North Star

Another Minnesota experiment station development, this fine little tree is a natural dwarf and consequently is used as a dwarfing stock for some other cherries. It is a good cherry in its own right, bearing good crops of juicy, sour red cherries of unusually good color and rosy-red juice. Despite its name, North Star is at home in warmer climes too, growing farther south than most sour cherries. Zones 4 to cooler parts of 8. Most nurseries list North Star.

Schmidt's Bigarreau

The group known as Bigarreau cherries have firm, brittle, sweet flesh, and are usually light-colored, as in Royal Anne, but Schmidt's Bigarreau is dark red. The fine-grained fruits are large, ripen in mid-June, and are borne in clusters. It is a pleasure to add that this is a hardy, strong-growing tree, deservedly popular with home gardeners. Zones 5 to 7. (Leuthardt)

Windsor

This good black sweet cherry is also extremely hardy; it originated in Canada. Even the flower buds are not easily killed by frost. The trees grow strongly, are known as good pollinators for other sweet cherries, and the medium-sized fruits with pink flesh are firm and of fresh-dessert quality. Ripening is in later June. Zones 5 to 7. (Leuthardt)

APRICOTS

If you want a fruit tree that will keep on pretending it is an ornamental even after its blossoms are gone, plant an apricot. It is an attractive tree that looks like a particularly handsome plum tree, with roundish, shiny green leaves. It is related to the plum, too, and also to the peach, and you can graft a plum scion or peach scion onto an apricot tree, or the other way around.

There have even been successful crosses of a plum as one parent and an apricot as another, the resulting fruit being called a plumcot. Luther Burbank did it first, and was regarded quite fishily by the horticultural community until more orthodox and less controversial plant breeders later managed to do the same thing. Burbank was pleased with his accomplishment, but in the end the plumcot was a curiosity rather than a desirable new fruit.

The apricot's historical home is central and western Asia, and it was known in China in 2200 B.C. Alexander the Great is supposed to have fetched it to Greece. It moved on to Italy, and Pliny mentioned it about 2000 years ago. In Colonial America apricots found a foothold in Virginia, and were brought to Spanish California by missionary priests.

The apricot is rather dry eating for some, although a fully tree-ripened apricot is juicy enough to please most tastes. The great majority of people know apricots only as a dried fruit, but this fruit dries so well that even a home gardener might want to dry some of his apricot crop if it is a bumper one. To do so, split the fruit, remove seed, pour boiling water over the fruits and let them stay in it for 20 minutes. Then drain off the water and place the halves of apricots, cut sides up, on cooky sheets and dry them for from 12 to 30 hours in the oven, starting at 125° F. for about four hours, then going to 155° F., and finishing at 125° F. for the last two hours or so. The high-temperature period should be about two thirds of the total time, and the apricots are done when they feel like soft leather. You can store them in plastic bags at a cool room temperature for months. We have kept them two years without deterioration.

Climate

Apricots constantly rush the season, which is fine if there isn't a late frost to kill their blossoms and wipe out that year's crop. If they can avoid that calamity they will thrive where most peaches thrive. If your site has good air drainage—a slope that runs downhill toward the north —it will go a long way to avoid spring frost damage.

The type of soil for apricots is not critical as long as it is well drained, for they will mope if grown in soggy spots.

Although they are more apt to be hurt by spring frosts than other fruit trees, they are not at home in a mild climate, and need some cold to break dormancy.

Pruning

Prune your apricot trees in the vase shape, like peaches. The trees' lively growth makes for a good deal of pruning. But unlike most peaches, apricots bear fruit on spurs. The spurs last for about three years, and by pruning away some inside branches you keep sunlight coming into the tree and stimulate it into growing new spurs to replace old ones. Even though grown on dwarfing cherry rootstocks, apricot trees may want to grow taller than you want them to. The remedy is to ruthlessly cut the tallest branches back to outward-pointing shoots.

Pollination

Most apricots are self-fruitful (though you'll get more fruit from each by growing two varieties).

Harvesting

To get a good harvest, once the fruits have formed, thin them unmercifully to 3 inches or 4 inches apart before they are an inch wide. The average apricot will set at least three times as much fruit as it can develop to proper size, so that without thinning it will wear itself out producing undersized fruits and then form none at all the following year.

Apricots will ripen if picked slightly green, and some fanciers of the fruit prefer this. Most, though, wait until the fruit is tree-ripe and sugary. The test for ripeness is: Twist the fruit slightly and it will come free if ripe. Handle it gently and the fruit will keep for two or three weeks in a cool place, but check the stored fruit frequently lest it over-soften.

Pests

Apricots are not often bothered by pests, and if pests appear, the more likely ones will be borers, brown rot, curculio beetles, and scale.

See Chapter 3 for descriptions and controls, Chapter 10 for sources of and further information on controls.

Varieties

Chinese Golden

The large freestone fruits are a lovely yellow with a reddish blush. Flesh is juicy for an apricot, and quality is good. Zones 5 to 8. (Burpee)

Early Golden

Pale orange, and freestone, this is a fairly new variety. Fruits are medium large and of good flavor when fully tree-ripe. Zones 5 to 8. (Boatman, Kelly, and Mellinger)

Golden Giant

This plum-size (2 inches across) apricot is a beautiful golden-orange fruit with exceptionally good flavor—

tender and juicy, a fresh-dessert apricot. Zones 5 to 8. (Interstate)

Henderson

A high-quality freestone, quite hardy and a good bearer. Fruits are yellow, blushed red. Zones 5 to 8. (Field)

Hungarian

Let this variety ripen fully on the tree to bring out its quality—considered one of the best. Fruits are large, and the tree is not as apt to over-bear as other apricots may. Zones 5 to 8. (Interstate)

Moorpark

One of the oldest varieties, Moorpark came from England. It is a large apricot, rich yellow flecked with red, the flesh juicy and consistently good. Zones 5 to 8. (Boatman, Burgess, Burpee, Kelly, Leuthardt, Mellinger, and Miller)

Superb

Originating in Kansas, this variety is said to be hardy and its firm orange-yellow fruits of good quality. Zones 5 to 8. (Interstate)

5

Dwarfs on Wheels

A little tree that will be a gorgeous bouquet each spring, a bountiful provider of mouth-watering fruit in summer —and one you can *also* move around anywhere you please like a piece of garden furniture—seems too good to be true. But it isn't. With a dwarf tree it *is* true. If dwarf fruit trees weren't made for growing in boxes, at least they are willing to pretend they were made for it, to accommodate themselves to it, and cheerfully grow their fruit in this highly unnatural situation.

True, there are some limitations, as you would expect. Not every dwarf fruit tree will do well in a box—or let's say a container, since there are various sorts. And those that will do well won't produce as much fruit as if they'd had the freedom of the open earth to root in. Also, they take more care, just as a bird in a cage takes more care than a chickadee feeding on your windowsill.

But if you can accept the minuses, some worth while

plusses are yours. For example:

• If you change houses, your little fruit tree in a container can move with you instead of languishing behind, permanently wedded to the open ground. This tree-moving is done quite a bit in England, perhaps because many house-holders in that garden-loving country lease rather than own their homes.

• Come winter cold, spring frost, fall frost, or ill-tempered winds, you can (and in fact should) shift your container-grown tree to more sheltered spots on your house grounds. This may save a whole season's crop, or it may extend the season, or permit you to grow a fruit that your climate has otherwise ruled out.

• When spraying is called for, you can move a container-grown tree to some spot that may be more convenient for the operation, and where you won't have to spray the house or whatever along with the tree.

• Because a fruit tree is a four-season beauty, lovely in blossom, foliage, fruit, and in its bare-branch pattern of winter, being able to move it also gives you the privilege of placing it where you can enjoy seeing it from the windows of your home during the cold months as well as from a garden lounge or hammock outdoors on terrace or patio during the growing season.

• And there is always the pure indulgence of moving for moving's sake—for the same reason you like to move furniture—just to see what it looks like in a different place. If so, we need say no more; container-grown dwarfs were made for you.

WHICH TREES WILL GROW WELL
IN CONTAINERS?

The rule for choosing the right trees here is simple and to the point: Choose the ones that will stay the smallest. In apples, the stempiece double-dwarfs are good bets for trees that will stay compact while giving you better harvests than you could expect from most other apple trees. In the case of the non-stempiece apple trees, the dwarfing rootstock should be EM 9, the same one we recommend for most apple trees planted in the open ground.

For pear trees, any variety will do, on the usual dwarfing rootstocks, but we particularly recommend Seckel if you can plant another pear nearby, either in a container or in the open ground; any other variety except Bartlett will do, as Seckel and Bartlett cannot pollinate each other. If you are limited to only one pear in a container and no other pear nearby, then Duchess is your girl, for she is self-fruitful. Her enormous fruits will need hard thinning the first two or three years so they won't strain the limbs of the young container-grown tree.

The new genetic peaches are ideal for container-growing. Bonanza and Starlet are the varieties. And the genetic dwarf Nectarina is the right container tree among nectarines.

Most dwarf plums will adapt to container planting, with dwarf Damsons particularly well sized for this purpose, and usually self-fruitful too. Among the European plums, good choices as pollination companions would be Green Gage and Stanley prune.

North Star cherry makes a good container plant, though some top pruning may be needed to keep the tree low. The crop from a container-grown cherry won't be much to talk about, but it is a pretty tree, and especially easy to protect from birds with a little netting when the crop is due.

Any dwarf apricot tree can be grown in a container.

One of the best dwarf trees for container planting, this Bonanza peach is already bearing a crop, although it is scarcely 2' tall.

Hungarian and Golden Giant are good choices if you have no special favorites.

WHAT ARE THE BEST CONTAINERS?

This may be the age of plastics but when it comes to

dwarf trees, wood remains the best material for a container. This is something reassuring about that, a calm indifference to vogue. Wood is porous enough but not too much, light in weight, non-shattering, durable, and a non-conductor of sun heat, which can harm roots in summer. So buy a wooden container, or cut a watertight wooden barrel in half, or get yourself some wood that is willing to endure a constantly moist situation; redwood, cedar, and cypress are all willing, and need no special treatment beforehand. Marine plywood is another possibility if it is at least a half inch thick. *Do not*, however, use a wood treated with creosote; it can and probably will kill your tree. The only preservative we know of that isn't suspect by *somebody* is Cuprinol. If you want to paint the outside of a container, use outside house paint, but don't paint it on the inside.

If you build your own container, a cube shape is simplest to make. For a dwarf tree's first two years, build the container to look approximately as shown in the drawing, making it 12 inches square and about 10 inches high. After two years of growing, the tree should be moved to a container 18 inches square and about 14 inches high. A strong-growing tree can use a container larger than this after about five years of growth, for example one that is 24 inches square and 20 inches high, or a half-barrel.

Use brass screws to make the cube containers. For trim and for extra strength, fasten one-by-two-inch strips at the top as shown, and also near the bottom, but not so low that they interfere with the wheels, if you use wheels. They are power-mower type, on axles running through a pair of two-by-fours fastened to the bottom of the container by their two-inch edges; their four-inch sides should be in line with the sides of the container. By curving the ends of the two-by-fours you can have runners, instead of wheels, on which the container can be moved by skidding it along. The same holes that serve to take the

HOME-MADE CONTAINER

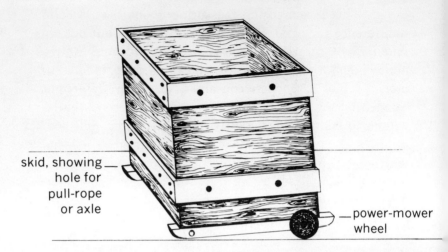

skid, showing —
hole for
pull-rope
or axle

— power-mower
wheel

axles for wheels can be used to pass a pull-rope through for skidding the container. For proper drainage, bore six half-inch holes in the floor of the container.

To move a readymade container you can make a dolly out of a square of heavy plywood by nailing two pieces of two by four on it and fastening heavy-duty castors to them as shown in the drawing. We suggest you use such a dolly only for moving the container, rather than as a permanent stand for it, because drainage will soon corrode the castors.

A half-barrel container should be held off the ground by placing four bricks, lying on their sides, under it. The bottom of the barrel, not the staves, should rest on the bricks. A half-barrel is not as conveniently moved as the other containers, but if done, a good way is to use three 4-foot lengths of 1½-inch dowels, such as the type that is sold for closet clothes poles. Start by levering the barrel up high enough to slide out two of the bricks it is resting on, and let the barrel come down on one of the dowels laid on the ground. Repeat this with the other two bricks and a dowel. The barrel can then be gently rolled on the dowels. As the barrel advances, keep picking up the

HALF-BARREL CONTAINER

under-side of dolly
using castors

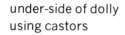

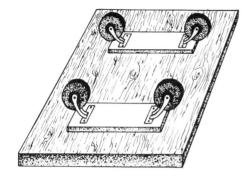

ready-made redwood
container

brick

dowel to the rear as soon as it is free of the barrel, and replacing it under the front of the barrel. This rolling is best done on a smooth and paved surface, or over two by fours laid as tracks, and is a two-man job—but easier than dragging the barrel.

WHAT PLANTING MIXTURE IS BEST?

We like to use as natural a mixture as we can for the tree in a container, so we usually use two parts of good garden soil and one part of compost.

We start by wetting the container well with a hose so the planting mixture will not lose its moisture to the wood.

Before putting the planting mixture in the container, cover the drainage holes with chunks of charcoal. If the planting mixture has some lumps in it, put them at the bottom. A little coarseness in the mixture is good, and the mixture should also be moist enough so that a squeezed handful will momentarily hold its shape in your hand.

No fertilizer is added when the tree is first planted, but the next year, in late winter or early spring, and each year thereafter, follow the program given below.

HOW TO PLANT THE TREE

Start by filling the container 1/3 full of the planting mixture. Then hold the tree suspended in the container at a point where the graft union will be slightly above the top of the container, and add more planting mixture, enough so the tree can stand by itself. For a stempiece apple tree, set it in the container so that its ground-level line will be about 3 inches below the container top. Next, using a piece of broomstick, tamp the planting mixture firmly about the roots, being careful not to change the position of the tree. Then set a stake and fasten the tree to it, unless it will be in a spot sheltered from winds. For better support, the stake can be nailed to one side of the container before the container is filled; some gardeners provide support for these newly planted trees by nailing two supports, one on each side of the container, and holding the tree between them.

Finally, fill the container to within 2 inches of its top. This 2-inch clearance provides a basin for watering the tree, which should be done now, using a compost solution. A layer of peat moss in the basin will provide a welcome mulch, and after the first year or two, compost makes an excellent mulch.

PRUNING

Prune as directed for the species in Chapters 2, 3, and 4, but give container trees harder pruning, and keep them under 5 feet tall. Pinching off tips of young growth in summer, when it is as long as your finger, is a good way to do this pruning as the trees mature.

WATERING AND FERTILIZING

Water evaporates through the sides and bottom of a container as well as from the soil surface, so these little trees need frequent watering. Plan on giving them a thorough soaking every week in dry spells. A top-watering with a spray will help from time to time, too, especially if the leaves are dusty.

Container trees usually need no more fertilizing than those which can search the earth for nutrients, because the container tree is kept smaller. Follow the fertilizing program according to species and age given in Chapter 3. If the container tree grows leaves at the expense of fruit, either cut the amount of fertilizer in half, or use cottonseed meal instead of blood meal. If, on the other hand, the container tree is not growing well, use compost solution for every other watering until matters improve.

FRUIT THINNING

Thin fruits of container trees more drastically than others. This thinning is necessary even with fruits that need no thinning when trees are in the open ground. Thin apple, pear, peach, and nectarine trees to a final total of eight or ten fruits the first bearing year; each year thereafter you can increase this total by half a dozen fruits. Apricots, European plums, and Japanese plums, on the other hand, can be allowed to ripen twice as many fruits. Damson plums and cherries should have one fourth of their fruits thinned in their first bearing year, one eighth the second bearing year, and none thereafter.

REPOTTING

When you move container trees to a larger container, do so in early spring before growth has started. The day before, give the tree a good watering. The day of repotting, spread a tarpaulin, drop cloth, or old shower curtain on the ground and put the container on it, laying it on its side. Loosen the earth from the sides of the container by sliding a handsaw blade down along the container sides. Then take hold of the base of the trunk, tap the sides of the container with a mallet, and slide the tree and its earth gently out. This is usually best done by two people—one pulling the tree while another holds on to the container.

Using a 3-pronged hand cultivator, remove about one third of the earth mixture from the sides and bottom of the root ball. Prune back larger roots by one third. Then repot the tree in fresh planting mixture, and in a larger container if it is due to move. We don't disinfect an old container before repotting, although we look it over to see that all is well inside.

When a container tree grows beyond easy potting, the usual course is to retire it to the open ground, perhaps as a garden ornament since it will be less productive and also smaller than other dwarfs because of the pruning given it and because container growing is itself a dwarfing process. However, you can keep a mature container dwarf going along in its later years without repotting by removing the top 4 to 6 inches of soil each year or two, pruning off exposed roots, and refilling with fresh soil mixture. This is a second-best measure, of course, but gardeners sometimes get so sentimental about these little trees, they can't bear to put them out to pasture.

6

How to Grow
a Living Sculpture

One of the nicest things you can do for your home is to
train a little dwarf fruit tree as an espalier—perhaps
against one wall of the house, or as an architectural accent at the front entrance, or as a screen for beauty and
privacy, or . . . Well, there are all sorts of beautiful
things you can do with espaliers, all sorts of shapes and
designs they are willing to grow into to please you.

And if you get into espaliering you'll be entitled to
feel pleasantly traditional, even historical. For the art of
espaliering is an old one, dating back to the Middle Ages
in Europe. The word itself comes from the Italian word
for support, *spalliera*, which in turn derives from *spalla*,
shoulder, and indeed certain forms of espaliers suggest
series of shoulders in their joined horizontals and ver-
ticals.

Before we go any further, let us say at once that espaliering need not be done for looks alone. It took hold in
Europe because it was also a practical way to grow fruit.
An espalier is confined to one plane. It can grow upward,
and from left to right, but not in other directions, or not

enough to matter. Thus, an espalier grown in the lovely candelabrum form may be about 6 feet high and 5 feet wide, but perhaps only 8 inches thick.

Yet in this narrow plane it occupies, an espalier can grow a surprising lot of fruit. A mature pear or apple tree grown in the candelabrum form may bear up to 100 pounds of fruit each season.

Another advantage of the espalier that the early practitioners of the art realized was its efficient use of sunlight. The light easily penetrates such a tree, encouraging growth of fruit spurs, and helping to ripen the fruit. Thus, espaliers have been deservedly popular with dwellers in regions of scanty sunshine.

And, since the entire tree is so much in the open and easily seen, the espalier can be tended—sprayed, pruned, and so on—with less effort.

For some reason, too, espaliers have a name for long life. We don't know why this is, unless the added attention and interest they receive plays a part, but even usually short-lived trees such as peach have been known to go on and on as espaliers, bearing regular crops far beyond their usual life span.

It may also be of interest to note that some American commercial fruit men are turning to espaliers for practical production, just as European growers have for centuries. The Americans use less hand labor—by pruning with power saws, for instance—but the lesson is implicit; espaliers are efficient producers, permitting so many more trees per acre that the tonnage per acre zooms.

WHICH ARE THE BEST TREES
FOR ESPALIERS?

Apples and pears are the trees most ideally suited for this training. They bear their fruit on long-lived spurs, and spurs are compact and thus well-fitted for a compact form. Apples and pears are sturdy trees and of steady growth, too. Another point in their favor is the large size of the fruits, so that production amounts to something. By contrast, an espaliered cherry tree would have too small a crop to please many owners, as would some plums. Among the best apple and pear varieties for espaliers are Cox's Orange Pippin apple, double-dwarf Golden Delicious apple, and Tyson pear.

Nevertheless, you *can* espalier any of the fruit trees we cover in this book. It is purely a matter of choice, once you understand the reasons for recommending the apple and pear.

Whatever the tree you choose, for espaliering purposes you can buy it as a whip, which is a single stem without any branches. This is a year-old plant and may cost less than an older tree. It is the right one to use for the cordon espaliers, which consist of a single branch grown in a vertical, an oblique, or a horizontal line. But if your little tree has some branch growth, you can remove the branches, or work with them for the other espalier forms if they are well placed.

TRAINING AN ESPALIER—THE SUPPORT

To train an espalier, you start out by building a support behind it, a kind of simple, sturdy trellis to which you can fasten the branches as they grow out, to make them point in the directions you wish. The trellis can be a permanent part of the espalier, though it is sometimes discarded after the tree is a few years old, has grown a strong framework, and is permanently set in its pattern.

You can make a trellis very much as you would make a grapevine support, by setting posts and stringing strong galvanized wire, about 14-gauge, between the posts. Include turnbuckles so you can take up slack in summer, and loosen the tension in winter. The lowest wire should be a foot from the ground, and wires should be spaced a foot or more apart up the posts. The number of wires depends on how tall the espalier will be. A horizontal cordon would need only one wire, while a Belgian fence

Already carrying a crop, this young apple is being trained as a single-U espalier, and is being allowed to grow taller than usual in order to cover a problem wall. Note that the fruits are borne on short laterals arising from the two main stems.

Three wires are being used as a support for this dwarf apple being trained in an informal palmette espalier as part of a fruiting fence. Note the heavy set of apples already formed on the first (lowest) arms. Note also the use of a straw mulch, and the metal trunk protector.

would need about three, and a single-U candelabrum, five or so.

If you prefer, a wooden framework can be used instead of the wires. Make it light but strong, using bamboo or the strips sold by lumberyards for trelliswork. To fasten a trellis to the side of your house or garage, use brackets and allow a one-foot space between trellis and wall. If yours is a hot-summer climate, try to choose a west or southwest wall in this case. A south wall will be too hot except in cool or cloudy climates; a north wall is not sunny; an east or southeast wall is possible but isn't quite right for ripening fruit well, and it may encourage frost damage in spring.

Wooden spring-type clothespins make good temporary clamps to hold branches to the support. Raffia makes a good and a good-looking tie that will last for a season. Old nylon stockings, while not much to look at, are really very good for tying, and plastic clips and Twist-ems are good ties. Whatever you use, don't spare the ties; use plenty. After a branch accepts the position, you can hold it snugly to the support with a single tie.

The design of the trellis will follow whatever shape the espalier is going to be. We will deal here with four espalier forms, illustrated by the drawings: the horizontal cordon, the Belgian fence, the candelabrum, and the palmette.

TRAINING AN ESPALIER—THE PRUNING

In addition to supporting an espalier, the other necessity is the pruning. This is an interesting job that takes frequent attention, and you can see why: In a nutshell, the tree wants to grow one way and you want it to grow another way. You make it do so with two kinds of pruning:

> 1. While the espalier is taking shape, snip off almost half of the previous season's terminal growth on framework branches early each spring; this is to encourage new shoot growth on the main framework during the training period, when you want a selection of other branches to form the design; after the espalier is mature, cut off *all* such terminal growth each spring, to maintain the mature shape. On growth other than the main framework branches, this spring pruning of terminal shoots from the previous season should reduce them to stubs a few inches long, to encourage the formation of fruit-bearing wood (spurs).

2. The other pruning is done during the growing season, usually June through August; it
consists of pinching back side shoots on all
branches, again to encourage development of
spurs. By "pinching back" we don't mean
pinching off. A good general rule is this: When
a side shoot (meaning any shoot growing from a
framework branch) gets to be several inches to
a foot long, pinch off about half of it. This will
make it grow out again from a bud. Then when
this *new* growth is about 6 inches long, pinch it
back enough to let it keep about two leaves.
Repeat this later in the season if the shoot
grows enough to make this necessary. Don't remove any spurs themselves, of course. They will
be found growing between vigorous shoots; and
because they are gnarled and stubby, they are
easily recognized once you get acquainted.

Since peaches and nectarines ordinarily bear their
crops not on spurs but on shoots a year old, you prune the
espaliered forms as follows:

In the spring, cut back terminal growth of
framework branches as already described for
other fruits. Then handle the side shoots in this
way: Remove about one out of three of them entirely, selecting the overgrown ones; next, short-
en half of the remaining side shoots to stubs
with two or three buds to grow wood for the following year's crop; finally, shorten the rest of
the side shoots by only a few inches, and they
will bear the current crop of fruit.

It is not necessary to do summer pruning on espaliered peach and nectarine trees except to maintain good
design or to remove dead or unhealthy wood.

THE ESPALIER FORMS

Of the espalier forms covered here, the candelabrum and the palmette are most suitable for peach and nectarine trees. Select a non-genetic dwarf peach or nectarine for espaliering purposes.

Horizontal Cordon

A horizontal cordon can be grown as low as 18 inches from ground level for a low path edger or bed divider, and if grown 3 feet from ground level it makes a most attractive border for a driveway or walk. An apple is the preferred tree for this use, and an unbranched whip is best to start with.

The support is a single wire strung between posts and placed about as high above the ground as you plan to grow the cordon. Posts should also be close to this height. Place one post just behind the spot where you are going to plant the tree, and place the other two posts in line, 6 feet on either side of the first post. String a wire between posts at the proper height.

After you plant the tree, cut off its top to slightly below the wire. This will force shoot growth from any buds below the cut. Select two good shoots, one to the right and one to the left, and as they grow out, bend each of them gently and tie it to its wire. These two horizontal branches will become your permanent framework. Each will grow to about 6 feet long. Keep all other growth on the *trunk* rubbed off with your finger while it is still in bud stage, in order to let all the strength go into the two arms.

Also keep pinching off any shoots along the arms that want to grow straight upward at their bases—and there will be a good many. The place for leaves and fruit spurs is on the *sides* and *bottom* of the framework branches. Encourage the development of spurs on the well-placed shoots by doing the summer pruning already described.

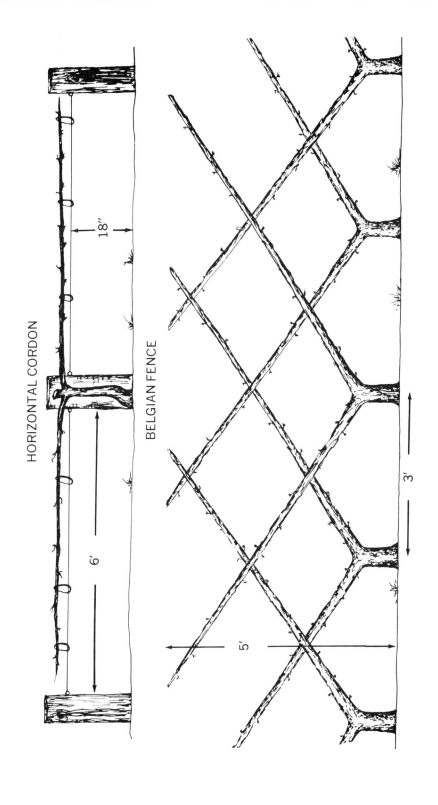

HORIZONTAL CORDON

18"

6'

BELGIAN FENCE

3'

5'

As simple a form as it is, the horizontal cordon is a good fruit producer for the space it takes. As gardeners know, making a branch grow horizontally encourages flowering.

Belgian Fence

This simple and entrancing pattern is made up of a row of trees planted 3 feet apart, and each trained in a Y-shape, the arms extending at 45-degree angles. The result is a series of diamond-shaped openings, each bordered with leaves in summer and in winter standing out in bare-branched relief. The Belgian fence makes a splendid screening planting—as a fence, as a summer garden wall, or as an enclosure for a veranda or a work area. Pear trees are especially good for this purpose, but any of the fruit trees covered in this book can be used.

Training is easy. After planting, cut each tree off 12 inches above the graft union, which will make side shoots grow out. Select one on each side, approximately at the same level above ground, and train them upward at 45-degree angles. Hold them there by tying them to temporary stakes and fasten the stakes to three wires strung one, three, and five feet above the ground. When trees are mature, they can be tied directly to the wires.

Don't let trees grow higher than the 5-foot wire. When they reach this point you can tie the terminal growth horizontally to the top wire, which will increase fruit production.

Candelabrum

This more elaborate form of espalier is perfectly suited to grow against the side of a house, where it is a breathtaking sight—and adds respectably to the attraction and value of the property. Pear and apple trees are very good for this form.

To make a single-U candelabrum espalier, after planting the tree, cut it off about 12 inches above the graft union, as with the Belgian fence espalier. Also as with the Belgian fence, the two best shoots on each side at about the same height are allowed to grow upward at a 45-degree angle the first season. This produces stronger

SINGLE-U CANDELABRUM

wood than if you immediately started to train them horizontally. But at the end of this first season, tie the two young limbs to their support in a horizontal line, bending them gently but firmly. Then bend the free end of each one to point straight up, and tie it to the support. The horizontal section should be about 6 inches long for each of the two arms.

Next spring you will start the vertical training by pruning back part of the terminal growth, as already explained, to induce strong new growth from buds. To keep the vertical arms rising symmetrically, you do this: If you use the growth from a bud on the outside of each arm this year, then use buds on the inside of each the following year, and so on until the form is mature.

As training continues, rub off any shoots on the lower trunk, and any that sprout at the top of this trunk where you pruned it off at planting time.

Palmette

The palmette is the least demanding of espaliers, since its form is simply a normal tree-shape in a single plane. Apple trees do very well in this shape, and are sometimes grown along a fence as palmettes.

To train a palmette, prune the tree at planting time to within 18 inches of ground level. Then select three good shoots of the new growth that will result from this pruning. One fairly vertical shoot and one at each side of it will give a good balanced shape. Rub off any others that sprout on the lower trunk. During the first season pinch back to two or three buds any shoots that attempt to extend the tree in wrong directions. Pinching back, not off, will encourage formation of spurs on these shoots.

In early spring before the start of the second season, prune back each of the main branches by one third or more. This will produce a lot of new wood and give you a good selection of permanent branches. Repeat this pruning the following year if it is needed. A palmette is considered mature after three years.

FERTILIZING AND WATERING ESPALIERS

Espaliers may need a little more fertilizing than other dwarf trees. Follow the directions in Chapter 3, and increase the amounts of fertilizer by about one quarter if the espaliers are not growing well.

Watering should be thorough, particularly while trees are getting established their first season. A mulch of compost, or of straw on top of a compost layer, will both nourish the trees and conserve moisture.

PALMETTE

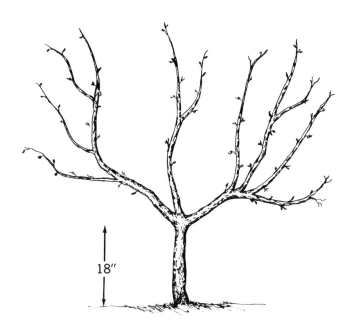

18″

WINTER DAMAGE

When you grow an espalier against a wall, the reflected heat on warm winter days may injure the tree's tender bark during its first three years, so give some protection to the trunk and partway up larger limbs. A foil wrapping will do it, but a coat of whitewash looks better.

7

The Collector's Fruit Garden—
The Delightful, The Different, and The Ancient

Of all the pleasures an amateur fruit gardener may enjoy, none eclipses the quiet delights of a vintage fruit-tree collection—one concerned with the ancient, the choice, the curious, the archetype. If racing has been the sport of kings, fruit growing has been a kingly pastime, and one of the best apples the world has known, White Winter Calville, was in King Louis XIII's garden at Orleans in the early 1600s. Louis also esteemed the exquisite Christmas apple, little Lady. Other apples were old when the Revolutionary War was flaming in America, and there are ancient pears and peaches. The good Agen plum was brought into Europe by Crusaders returning from the Holy Land, and a fine cherry, Yellow Spanish, is believed to be some *two thousand* years in cultivation.

To grow the very fruit that Roman emperors relished, or that Thomas Jefferson once hand-tended at Monticello, or that the first Queen Elizabeth dallied with, somehow confers a special *eclat.*

But age alone is not the be-all and end-all. These venerable varieties have endured because they are choice.

Indeed, it is mystifying why they are not widely grown today, unless we admit there exists a sometimes preposterous human fickleness. However, there does seem a good possibility that home fruit gardeners, as a rule, simply don't know that these fascinating kinds of apples, pears, and so on exist—or where to get nursery stock if they have heard about any of them.

For this reason, as in Chapter 4, we give sources for each variety that follows. In many cases the source is Southmeadow Fruit Gardens, a small and specialized enterprise in Michigan begun by Mr. Robert A. Nitschke, a private collector of choice fruits. Here and there we have quoted him on some characteristics of a variety he has had under observation for years.

Another outstanding American nursery in this rare-variety field is Leuthardt, on Long Island. Like Southmeadow, they make a specialty of dwarf trees.

In a few cases we have also included as a candidate for the collector's garden a species plant not often or widely grown for its fruit, yet deserving of better acquaintance and appreciation.

APPLES

Ashmead's Kernel

This old English apple was named for the Gloucester physician who first grew it from a seed two centuries ago, and a good job it was. The skin is a yellowish brown russet, and the yellowish flesh is sweet and delicious, with an aromatic quality of the highest order. Dr. Ashmead's apple ripens late in October and keeps well all winter and into spring. (Southmeadow)

Black Gilliflower

George Washington may have eaten this old apple, also called Sheepnose, for it dates back to at least the

Revolutionary War. So dark red as to be almost black, this variety is noted also for the delightful fragrance of the fruits and the aromatic flavor of the crisp greenish flesh. The apples ripen in November and have the good habit of not dropping. Another point to note is that they keep very well in ordinary cool-basement storage if they are harvested before they pass their peak of ripening. (Leuthardt and Southmeadow)

Calville Blanc D'Hiver

In translation, the White Winter Calville, this exquisitely good and quite old apple is still the darling of France, where King Louis XIII had it in his Orleans gardens more than 300 years ago. Like so many supremely choice fruits, it is not a beauty to look at—ridged and uneven, a greenish ground color dotted with red—but when perfectly grown and ripened, the delicately spicy flesh is without equal. Mr. Nitschke notes that a sunny site is imperative for proper ripening, and that the fruits attain full perfection only after the second or third harvest year, a peculiarity that should merely endear Calville to the collector. Ripening, as with nearly all superb apples, is late, here as late as November. (Leuthardt and Southmeadow)

Chenango Strawberry

Too delicate to go to market, this delightful early September apple was discovered in New York state several years before the Civil War. Its merits recommended it widely, and the fruit expert U. P. Hedrick noted in the Cyclopedia of Hardy Fruits: ". . . It now grows in the orchard of nearly every amateur applegrower." Beautiful and fragrant as well as luscious, Chenango must be picked at the exact right time, "just as the skin begins to develop a milky appearance," Mr. Nitschke says, if the flesh is to hold its juicy, perfect taste. (Leuthardt and Southmeadow)

Cox's Orange Pippin

This famous English apple sprouted from a seed of the also famous Ribston Pippin, and soon became a pet of England's apple gourmets. Its medium-sized fruits, splashed with orange-red on a deep yellow background, give but little hint of the delights of its melting, mellow-tinted flesh of highest quality. Although this prince of apples has not always grown well in the United States— and is still little-known here—Mr. Nitschke reports from Michigan that it does beautifully there in his climate, ripening toward the end of September. (Leuthardt and Southmeadow)

Dr. Matthews

If you ever wondered whether any apple was named for the profession that apples are supposed to keep at bay, this variety may settle the matter. And another old variety was called plain "Doctor." At any rate, the Dr. Matthews apple, named for whom we haven't any idea, was widely known and liked in Indiana earlier in this century for its sprightly flavor and unusually good keeping qualities. Ripening fairly early, September, it will keep until late the following spring. (Southmeadow)

Early Joe

As if to keep from spoiling gardeners, nature often seems to combine epicurean quality in fruit with certain troublesome traits, and so it is here. Early Joe, ripening in August, is one of the best early apples ever grown—but the tree is not a willing bearer, produces a good many runty apples, and is susceptible to scab. But Early Joe has some pear-like flavor and is crisp, juicy, and tender.

It originated from an apple seed planted in 1800 in New York state. (Southmeadow)

Esopus Spitzenburg

If you can grow this finicky apple, which is often terribly particular about soil and climate and is susceptible to scab, you will have a prize. It is an old American fruit, originating in New York State 200 or more years ago, and is so good—tart, spicy, and aromatic—that it became known lovingly to critical European connoisseurs as "Spitz." The handsome apples are shaped much like the familiar Red Delicious, and keep just as well as it does. Spitz is colored a warm red on a yellow background, as pretty as it is good. It ripens late, from late October to early November. (Leuthardt and Southmeadow)

Fameuse

So white is the crisp flesh of this old Canadian apple that "Snow apple" is another name for it. Sometimes the flesh is lightly streaked with red. Fameuse is said to have originated from one of several seeds sent from France. It is a cold-country apple, ripening in October, but not a really good keeper. The trees are somewhat temperamental about the soil they will grow in, but these little apples have nevertheless been most highly thought of over the three centuries or so that they have been known. (Kelly, Leuthardt, and Southmeadow)

Freyberg

Imagine a cross of the remarkably good Cox's Orange Pippin and fine Golden Delicious. There is such an apple, and its name is Freyberg. Modern by apple standards, this delicious little yellow apple with sweetly tart, creamy white flesh, ripens early in October and is so good that its devotees seem to despair of a worthy comparison,

calling its taste a combination of pear, apple, banana
. . . even a hint of anise. (Southmeadow)

Golden Russet

Dating back at least 150 years to some unknown ori-
gins, this exceptionally fine sweet apple gained the good
reputation of being little bothered by pests—a tempting
recommendation even if it wasn't a first-class dessert
apple. But it is, and has the added merit of keeping
beautifully all winter long in ordinary basement storage.
It ripens in late October or sometimes later. (Kelly,
Leuthardt, and Southmeadow)

Golden Sweet

This is an early yellow apple, starting in August to
ripen over several weeks. Dating from the early nineteenth century, its sweet firmness made it a popular
home-garden variety that was once widely grown, and it
deserves to be better known to today's home gardeners.
(Southmeadow)

Irish Peach

This old Irish apple is, appropriately, green. The
green is faintly striped with red, and the fruits ripen very
early—in July. The flavor is rich and good, a fine dessert
apple. In his book, *The Anatomy of Dessert*, the English
gourmet Edward Bunyard advised eating Irish Peach
right off the tree to best enjoy its "fresh acidity with
slight spicy aroma." (Southmeadow)

Jefferis

This fine old early fall apple is a good example of the
kind of fruit no one but a home gardener is ever apt to
taste. The reason is, Jefferis disqualifies itself for market

on several counts—fruits are not well colored, are neither large nor uniform, and they ripen unevenly. But none of these points is important in the home fruit garden, especially when you taste the tender, rich flesh, nicely tart, with a pear-like lusciousness. (Southmeadow)

Jonalicious

This late September apple is a recently introduced variety, a hybrid of Jonathan and Red Delicious, and may be the best of the several offspring from the combination. It somehow resembles in flavor the delightful Cox's Orange Pippin, although there is no known relationship. (Stark)

Knobbed Russet

This is an ugly duckling of an English apple, appearing to go out of its way to look unappealing—streaked and blotched, and marked with warty knobs. The reason it was not allowed to die out long ago (it dates back to the Napoleonic era) is its superb quality under that homely skin, making it one of the most esteemed of winter dessert apples among those who know it. (Southmeadow)

Lady

These little fruits, no larger than a crab apple, are so pretty that they are in demand for Christmas decorations as well as for holiday dessert. Lady also has a name as one of the finest eating apples, although in our experience it must be carefully grown to attain this quality. Lady is quite an old apple and was one of the favorites of that royal epicure Louis XIII of France. "Pomme d'Apis" is another name for Lady. It is a late apple, ripening in November and making a beautiful sight as a dwarf tree laden with the beautiful, rather flattened, little red and buttery-yellow fruits. (Kelly, Leuthardt, and South-meadow)

Lady Sweet

If you prefer a non-tart apple, this is a choicely good one. Lady Sweet became a popular apple in the Midwest and East during the Nineteenth century after the famous fruit authority Andrew Jackson Downing singled it out for excellence in 1845. The medium-large apples are attractively striped, and the harvest season is November. Lady Sweet is a heavy bearer and a good keeper. (Southmeadow)

Lamb Abbey Pearmain

This old English apple with the interesting name was the seedling offspring of an American apple, Newtown Pippin. Mid-season, ripening in September, this variety is an exceptionally good candidate for the home garden according to Mr. Nitschke, who finds it a regular and heavy bearer in Michigan. He describes the small red-striped apples as having sugary, yellowish-white, crisp flesh. (Southmeadow)

Late Strawberry

Because its fruits are small and do not ripen all at once, this apple has always belonged strictly to home gardeners, who aren't concerned about marketing problems. But Late Strawberry is a beautiful apple and has a wonderful quality of flesh, which is yellow, juicy, and aromatic. Ripening starts in September. (Southmeadow)

Lord's Seedling

This delicious morsel is an almost impossible apple to find, as it was one of many trees grown only for testing at the New York experiment station and was not, like nearly all such others, destroyed afterward. It has been growing at the station since 1892, and has never been considered an apple that would go anywhere commercially as it is yellowish with rusty blotches. But this plain little thing produces annual heavy crops of delectable apples in late August. (Southmeadow)

Margil

This is a quite old, red English apple, possibly borrowed from the French. It has been greatly prized as a dessert apple by such English connoisseurs as Edward Bunyard, who found it almost buttery in texture and believed it a probable ancestor of the great Cox's Orange Pippin and of Ribston Pippin. Margil ripens in late September. (Southmeadow)

Mother

A Massachusetts apple, first appearing in horticultural literature in 1848, this excellent red apple with a tart flavor all its own made a name for itself in England, but is hardly known anymore on this side of the Atlantic. Bunyard thought it one of the few American apples worth troubling with, though he felt the flavor would not appeal to everyone. Hedrick compared it to the fine Esopus Spitzenberg, but thought Spitz slightly better—which does little to detract from Mother. It ripens in September. (Southmeadow)

Muster

This old American apple, reddish-orange, sometimes pink, rather small and flattened, dates back into at least the mid-nineteenth century, but no one knows how old it really is or where it first grew as, no doubt, a seedling. When at its best, it has been rated by experts as one of the supremely good dessert apples. It ripens in early September. (Southmeadow)

Newtown Pippin

Known variously as Green Newtown, Albemarle, Mountain Pippin, Yellow Newtown, as well as by other names, this very old American apple belongs in the garden of any enthusiast who can promise it good soil, full sun, and a long warm summer. Thomas Jefferson was growing this variety at Monticello in 1778, and 19 years before that, some of the apples were sent to Benjamin Franklin in England because they were so good. Newtown was an ideal apple to last out such a long voyage without harm, for this fine apple is not only a good keeper but must be kept in storage a few months in order to develop top flavor, which comes toward the end of winter. That severe critic Hedrick called this old green apple's flavor the best of any, once it had reached its perfection. (Southmeadow)

Pitmaston Pineapple

If you are willing to overlook this old yellow apple's runty size, you will be rewarded by its exquisite taste— not particularly of pineapple, despite the name, but, in Bunyard's phrase: ". . . a remarkable blend of honey and musk." He added that it is worthy of a corner in any epicurean garden. Harvest is in early September. (Southmeadow)

Pomme Royal

This is an old French apple, known in the United States since Colonial times, and called variously Dyer, Golden Spice, and White Spice. The translucent, creamy flesh is so aromatic and spicily delightful, it has sent centuries of apple lovers into rhapsodies. The tree itself is inclined toward frailty, worse luck, and is a shy bearer as well as an every-other-year one, nor is it as long-lived as apple trees usually are. But at its best, Pomme Royale is so superb that if it does well for you, you will forgive its faults at each of its September harvests. (Southmeadow)

Red Gravenstein

This is a red sport of the famous Danish apple, and a very good one. It dates back to the eighteenth century, and is used for both fresh dessert and for cooking. The flesh is delicate, the size large. Bunyard found Gravenstein so aromatic that its very skin perfumed the fingers. Red Gravenstein ripens in late August. (Southmeadow)

Ribston Pippin

Just as American apples are often worthless when grown in the English climate, English apples frequently fail to succeed in America. But Ribston Pippin is different, normally doing well in the U.S. This reddish-orange apple with the rich and sprightly flavor was England's king of dessert apples until Cox's Orange Pippin became a serious rival. Ribston ripens in mid-September. According to Bunyard it is, at least in England, happiest when it can get its roots close to an abundant source of water, such as a river. (Leuthardt and Southmeadow)

Ross Nonpareil

This is a small red and brown Irish apple, quite old and perhaps of French origin. Though praised by some old-time connoisseurs as supremely good, the variety nearly died out, but was rescued in recent years by the Royal Horticultural Society in England. It ripens in early October. (Southmeadow)

Roxbury Russet

This excellent late winter apple was 150 years old when the Revolutionary War started, and even as recently as 50 years ago was still the best known russet apple in the country. But when cold storage came along, more attractive apples could be held for market all winter, even though they weren't as good eating as Roxbury Russet. For the home gardener, the fine keeping qualities, providing fresh apples as late as May, recommends this good old apple with the tough skin and the delicious, juicy yellow flesh. It ripens in October. (Leuthardt and Southmeadow)

Swaar

As its name suggests, this is a Dutch apple, although the Dutch in this case were early settlers of the Hudson River Valley, where this variety originated. The medium-large apples are not beautiful but have a delightful and rich flavor, to which Hedrick gave one of his rare "very good to best" ratings. The fruits ripen in early November, and keep very well in ordinary storage all winter. (Southmeadow)

Sweet Bough

This American apple was first described in horticultural literature in 1817, and in time became known as the best sweet summer apple, the handsome green fruits retaining their honeyed sweetness when cooked, as well as being prized for eating fresh. They ripen in late August. (Southmeadow)

Tydeman's Late Orange

Cox's Orange Pippin is one of the parents of this English apple, and the offspring does credit to its breeding. This is one of those apples which, like Newtown Pippin, develops its glorious peak of perfection in storage, attaining it a month or so after the November harvesting. Its red-and-yellow skin develops a warmer glow while stored, and the yellow flesh is suggestive of Cox but has a flavor of its own. (Southmeadow)

White Winter Pearmain

Early in the last century the pioneer settlers of Ohio and Indiana prized this October apple that kept well all winter and was one of the best dessert apples of all. It seems tempting to speculate if White Winter Pearmain might have been one of Johnny Appleseed's introductions, but the speculation is idle; this variety came into the territory as scionwood for grafting, toted by saddle-bag—and Johnny Appleseed was strictly a seedling man, with no use at all for propagation by grafts. (Southmeadow)

PEARS

Atlantic Queen

An old French pear, renamed by Leuthardt in recognition of its splendid adaptation to East Coast growing conditions, this variety recommends itself to the home gardener on two other scores, size and quality. Fruits weigh up to 1½ pounds, are borne in profusion, and quality is excellent—the fruits being juicy, sweet, and aromatic. The Queen is highly resistant to fire blight also. Fruits ripen in September in New York state. (Leuthardt)

Beurre Giffard

Here is a good and old pear that ripens in summer. The medium-large fruits keep well and have unusually small cores. The variety came from France, and at harvest time—early August—the fruit is pale yellow with a pink blush. The pears are ready to eat after a week on the

shelf for the usual after-harvest ripening of pears. (Southmeadow)

Beurre Superfin

This is another old French pear, a seedling grown in
1837 at Angers. It is one of the finest flavored of pears,
with a tender skin, too tender for shipping. It has long
been grown as a dwarf as it does well on dwarfing stock.
Harvest is in late September, and after-ripening takes
about a month. (Southmeadow)

Dr. Jules Guyot

This early pear has a bright yellow skin tinted with
pink, very pretty, and fruits are large. The quality is
high, with tender, melting flesh that is juicy, sweet, and
delicately flavored. Ripening is in August. (Leuthardt)

Doyenne Gris

This old pear was first grown near Paris about 1750,
and does well in U.S. pear country. It is a plump, medium-sized, golden brown fruit, its buttery flesh sweet
and spicy. Ready to pick in late September, its after-
ripening takes about a month. (Southmeadow)

Flemish Beauty

Although this fine pear has sometimes been too susceptible to scab and fire blight for comfort, if it should
prove healthy in your garden you would be very glad you
grew it. Hedrick praised its flavor as nicely balanced between sweet and tart, with great richness and an ap-
pealing muskiness. The variety was found early in the
nineteenth century as a chance seedling growing in a
wood in Belgium. (Southmeadow)

Niji Seiki

As round as an apple, and with mild and juicy apple-crisp flesh instead of the buttery flesh associated with pears, this Japanese variety is an interesting specimen for a home garden. In spring it blooms so profusely it is like a white bouquet, and the fruit set is consistently so heavy that hard thinning is needed to keep the size of the pears satisfactory. Ripening extends throughout September. (Southmeadow)

Sheldon

Though not so ancient as pears go—it grew from a seed planted about 1815, the year of the battle of Waterloo—Sheldon is old enough to have proved its superb quality over and over to generations of pear lovers. It is an apple-round pear, russeted and with a reddish cheek, the melting flesh so sweet and aromatic that Hedrick felt it merited the term "luscious" almost more than any other pear he knew. The trees could be more thrifty, and they need some protection from wind to avoid some loss of ripening fruits. Fruits may be picked, however, as soon as the first ones begin to fall, which is in October. (Southmeadow)

PEACHES

Belle of Georgia

This is a white-fleshed peach, with a complexion like an old-fashioned beauty—creamy white, blushed with bright red, and, surprisingly, not easily bruised. Old Belle has been sending peach lovers into lyrical delight for decades, and many swear and declare she is the best white peach on earth. She is also freestone to semi-cling, happily hardy, and not as easily harmed by late spring frosts as many other peaches. Ripening is in late August in the Midwest. (Boatman, Burpee, Hastings, Leuthardt, Savage, and Waynesboro)

Champion

Grown as a seedling tree in Nokomis, Illinois, in 1880, Champion grew from a seed of Oldmixon Free, and bore so good a fruit that it became a standard of excellence for white-fleshed peaches. The fruits are small and may not color well when the tree is grown in certain soils, but they are attractive, extremely tender, delicate, and sweet, and are freestone or semi-free. They ripen in mid-August. (Miller and Southmeadow)

Dwarf Chinese Peaches

There are two species of natural dwarf peaches that are of some interest to the serious collector, although neither bears peaches of top quality for eating fresh. Field lists the Flory peach, a shrub type that grows to 5 feet; it is nearly as ornamental in foliage as Bonanza (see Chapter 4), and bears white-fleshed freestone fruits, best used as cooking peaches.

Hastings lists Mandarin peach, smaller in growth habit than Flory, making more of a bush than a hedge plant. Like Flory, foliage is close-spaced and attractive, and fruits are similar to Flory in quality.

> *Note:* Because there are not many unusual peach trees in dwarf form, and because the height of a standard size peach tree can be held at 10 feet through pruning, we list below a group of five varieties in standard size that we cannot resist including. You will see why when you read the descriptions.

George IV

This is one of the first peaches that attained a notable

reputation in the United States—and is an American peach, despite its name. Hedrick dismissed it as supplanted by better peaches, but we include it here because another opinion, that of Mr. Nitschke, is so favorable to this variety: "If I were asked to name the most delicious peach I have ever tasted," he has said of this little greenish-white fruit, "I believe I would select George IV." He called its freestone white flesh "a perfect blend of sugary sweetness and perfumed acidity." Interestingly, George IV originated in a fruit garden on New York's Broad Street in Lower Manhattan, now the skyscrapered financial district. (Southmeadow)

Grosse Mignonne

This variety has been in cultivation for some 300 years—and this venerable record together with the excellent white-fleshed quality, juicy and rich, recommends Grosse Mignonne for the connoisseur's garden. The skin is usually greenish-white, and the fruits are medium-large. Harvest is in early September. (Southmeadow)

Late Crawford

Until Elberta captured commercial growers' favor with its larger production and showier appearance, this member of the Crawford group of peaches was America's No. 1 peach. Today, most people have never heard of a Crawford peach, but this variety, now close to 200 years old, is still available and, unusual for a once commercial variety, is a splendid one for the home garden. It is a delicious yellow-fleshed peach, its skin an attractive red and yellow. The variety has always had a good name for health and for adaptability to varying soils and climates. It is a late peach, ripening toward the end of September. (Southmeadow)

Oldmixon Free

The name of this old white peach, grown from a seed in 1800, apparently comes from that of the English historian, Sir John Oldmixon, who on a visit to America some time before 1742, brought some peach seeds along, one of which grew into the parent of this variety. The "Free" in the name is for the fruit's generally freestone character. It is white-fleshed, its skin a creamy white blushed and splashed with reds, and its flavor is exceptionally rich and fine. The tree blooms late enough to escape some late spring frosts. Though not as productive as some peaches, Oldmixon Free is a hardy variety, well worth growing. The fruits ripen late in September. (Southmeadow)

Slappey

We know neither where Slappey first appeared nor how it got its name, but it is an old and very good yellow-fleshed American peach with a clear flavor that Mr. Nitschke describes as "pine-like." The thin skin is so nearly fuzzless that this quality will recommend Slappey to many who wish peaches were like nectarines in this way. Ripening time is late August. (Southmeadow)

PLUMS

Agen

Known also as d'Agen, French Prune, and Petite Prune, this old violet-purple plum is grown extensively in California today to be dried for sale as a prune. It is an old variety, brought from the Near East during the Crusades. Though a commercial favorite, Agen is also a fine home garden plum, sweet and a consistently good cropper. Eaten fresh, it is luscious, and if you have a mind to make your own dried prunes, Agen will help by hanging so long on the tree that the curing can begin before the harvesting, which is ordinarily in late September. (Southmeadow)

General Hand

This choice golden-yellow plum is a European species, one of the Green Gage types, and was grown from seed on the home grounds of one General Hand of Lancaster, Pennsylvania. The original tree first bore fruit in 1790. The plums reach their perfection when allowed to ripen thoroughly before picking, and are then among the choicest of plums. Although not an abundant producer, General Hand deserves consideration by any home gardener who loves plums. It ripens in early September. (Southmeadow)

Imperial Epineuse

Even sweeter than the very sweet Agen, this large European plum, a prune type, was discovered 100 years ago in France, growing as a chance seedling. It is clingstone and has an attractive reddish-purple skin. Once a widely grown commercial variety in California but now supplanted by others, Imperial Epineuse remains a splendid home-garden fruit. The firm flesh is greenish-yellow, ripening in September. (Leuthardt and Southmeadow)

Jefferson

This beautiful and delicious orange-fleshed plum was raised in Albany, New York, from a seed of a European plum in 1825, and we'd like to think it was named in honor of Thomas Jefferson, who was still living at the time and was one of the best friends of home gardening. Hedrick called this fruit one of the best of all dessert plums. It fell out of favor with commercial growers because the trees are less hardy than some others and can grow well only in certain soils, and because the plums were too delicate for market use. Jefferson ripens about the middle of September. (Southmeadow)

Mirabelle

This term refers to a type of Damson plum. Small, rich yellow in color, these sweet little plums are much favored in France, which says a good deal for their high quality. They are also greatly esteemed for cooking. Ripening is generally in August. Three kinds of Mirabelles are offered: Leuthardt lists one under the type name, and Southmeadow lists Mirabelle de Nancy, and a hybrid of Petite Mirabelle and Imperial Epineuse called American Mirabelle.

Pearl

This is one of the many plums that Luther Burbank introduced, this one in 1898. Pearl was not hybridized, but was grown from a seed of Agen—as far as is known, Burbank being much more interested in results than in keeping close track of his fruits' bloodlines. Pearl is well named, its golden yellow fruits covered with a heavy white bloom and dotted with red. Its flavor also lives up to its looks; the deep yellow flesh is tender, sweet, and most delicious. Technically a prune, with prune sweetness, Pearl is too juicy to dry easily, and is most ideal as a fresh fruit. It ripens in September. (Southmeadow)

CHERRIES

Early Rivers

A very dark red, sweet cherry from England, this variety has the merit of seldom cracking in wet weather, and is one of the world's very good cherries. Referring to it, Bunyard grew lyrical: ". . . a large soft black fruit, sweet and very rich when well ripened. . . . To know Early Rivers, or indeed any other cherry, at its best, one must walk through the orchard a fortnight after the crop has been gathered, and here and there a fruit which has been missed will reveal to the gleaner what a cherry really may be." Early Rivers ripens early. (Southmeadow)

Governor Wood

This is a yellow-red sweet cherry, grown from a seed in 1842 by a physician and amateur breeder, Dr. Jared P. Kirtland, of Cleveland. Governor Wood is mild, sweet, and good, an excellent choice for a home collection. It ripens early. (Southmeadow)

Kirtland's Mary

The Dr. Kirtland who bred the Governor Wood cherry also originated this one, and named it for his daughter. The fruits are an interesting flesh-pink color and have one of the richest of all cherry flavors. (Southmeadow)

Yellow Spanish

This excellent red and yellow sweet cherry of the Royal Ann type is exceptionally fine—sweet and rich—and is interesting as a garden specimen because of its antiquity. Pomologists believe it traces back to the first century of the Christian era. For a fruit to remain in cultivation for 2000 years it must be very, very good, and Yellow Spanish decidedly is. Hedrick rated it "very good to best." A late-ripening cherry, it has been grown in America since 1802. Incidentally, birds are often less troublesome in the case of non-red cherries such as this one, apparently not realizing the fruits are ripe, because they are not red. (Southmeadow)

8

Success Tips

We were offering some garden seeds to a woman once, because we had a surplus of the seeds and she had a nice place in her yard to plant them. To our surprise she turned them down. "I've never grown these," she said, "so I wouldn't know how." We told her the plants needed just ordinary care.

"So *you* say," she said, giving us a knowing look, "but *I* know there are all kinds of little tricks to it, just the same."

This chapter is included because there was something to what she said. We don't like to think that gardening is a baffling enterprise—any gardening—but it is true that as with any adeptness, there are certain "little tricks" to it. Knowing some of the tricks helps.

GENERAL TIPS

When planting a fruit tree, some gardeners

*When a dwarf tree bears a heavy load of fruit, as this Golden
Delicious stempiece dwarf is doing, the effect is to "umbrella"
the tree, the weight of fruit bending the limbs toward the horizontal. They tend to remain in this general attitude, and this
is good, for it is the more lateral limbs that produce the most
fruit. The spreading of limbs also lets more sunlight into the
tree, helping to color the fruit, and inducing more spur growth.*

mix into the planting hole soil dug from around
another tree of the same species. When possible, they use soil in this mixture not only
from the same species, but from the same variety. They think that such sharing of soil and its
micro-organic population also helps a young
tree that may not be doing as well as it should.

• To encourage a leaf bud to grow (as when
you want it to begin forming a branch at a
place where the tree needs one), cut off all or a

part of the limb beyond the bud during spring pruning. This is called forcing. If you don't want to sacrifice the outward portion of the limb, do this: Cut a small notch in the limb immediately above the bud. The effect will be to slow the passage of nutrients toward the end of the limb. It is always the farthest-out growth that gets the most nutrients, carried there by the sap.

• Watersprouts, the vertical shoots that spring up in the center of a treetop in summer, are usually removed because they are seldom well-placed and they tend to keep sunshine out of the tree's interior. However, watersprouts are also a sign of tree vigor. If one is well located, you can allow it to remain. Bending it toward the horizontal, as explained next, will turn it into a working limb.

INDUCING BUD GROWTH BY NOTCHING

• If a branch that is too important to the tree to be pruned off is growing too upright, you can improve its posture, and at the same time encourage it to form more blossoms, by bending it down and holding it there for a month or more. Tie a rope to the branch and pull it gently down to a horizontal position or lower. Then anchor the rope to a peg in the ground, as illustrated.

Or insert a notched "spreader" stick between limb and trunk, as shown. Be sure the limb is flexible enough for either of these treatments, not more than 2 inches thick at its base.

• If the central leader of a dwarf tree is allowed to bear a heavy load of fruit during the

BENDING LIMB TO INDUCE FRUITING

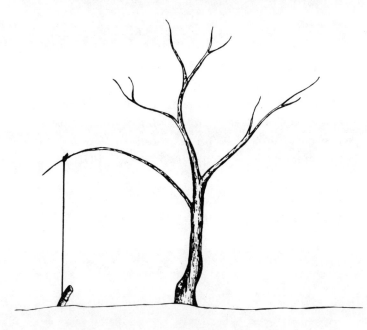

first two or three fruiting seasons, this will bend it down and will often result in stunting the tree. This stunting is not always unwelcome, though the tree is somewhat deformed as a result of the leader's bending.

• A tree grows upward by extending the *tips* of its branches. Thus, any place on the trunk, or any limb growing from the trunk, is the same height from the ground when the tree is 50

BENDING LIMB WITH A SPREADER TO INDUCE FRUITING

spreader

years old as when it was a year or two old.

• Too-vigorous growth of a tree can be quelled by pruning back the longer branches in July and August. Spring pruning *stimulates* vegetative growth, but summer pruning *stunts* it and also encourages fruit formation.

• The best time to prune an unwanted branch is when it is merely a tender young shoot. Simply pinch it off with your thumbnail. You can also halt the outward growth of a too-vigorous young branch by pinching off its tip.

• Prune your trees with a camera? Actually, a picture record of a fruit tree, starting with its first spring at planting time, will teach you more about pruning than anything else can. Take each year's picture from the same spot and on about the same date. In three years you will be able to see exactly what the tree did in response to what you did. Date the photographs and file them in manila envelopes, one envelope for each year. This way, you can take out the photographs of your fruit garden for several years running, line them up side by side, and see how the trees grew. On the face of each envelope write the significant information for that year; this will include mention of long dry or wet spells, late spring frosts, pest attacks, the amount and quality of the harvests.

A good accessory for this picture-taking is a 6-foot pole painted white and marked at one-foot intervals with black stripes. Stand it beside the tree when you take a picture.

Also keep in mind that a light-colored background will make your pictures clearer. A white or light-blue sheet is a good one, and will prevent a background of the branchy clutter that often obscures the details you want clearly shown. The side of a white house is also a good background if shadows do not interfere. And if you can take the photograph from a position near the ground, and aim upward, the sky can serve as background. Black-and-white photographs are the ones that particularly need attention to background simplicity, although color photographs and transparencies should be checked on this point before taking the picture.

• Dwarf apples on Malling rootstocks sometimes run into stress problems, such as a root rot, when a very hot and dry summer is followed by a very wet fall. If your climate often runs to this pattern, an apple tree dwarfed by means of a stempiece is more likely to succeed.

• If you should find yourself short of time when some spraying positively must be done, you might try doing what some commercial fruit growers are finding is a good new shortcut. They apply a spray to only one side of the tree, then put it on the other side later. The interval between the two sprays is a little longer than half the usual time lapse between sprays. If the usual interval between sprays is, say, two weeks, the fruit grower may spray the east side of his trees nine or ten days after he sprays the west side of them. The one-side spray covers up to 90 percent of a well-pruned tree, and has been successful in controlling scab and powdery mildew on apple trees.

• If you buy property with an old fruit tree on it, should you keep the tree, knowing that old fruit trees aren't supposed to be worth saving? It is true that most fruit trees wear out in time, producing smaller and less desirable fruits than when they were younger. Our feeling, though, is that an old tree has a right to live if it isn't hopelessly diseased or completely out of place for your purposes. To give it the best chance of bearing a pretty good crop, do this the first autumn: Scrape the trunk and larger limbs. Burn the scrapings. Scrub trunk and limbs with soapy water. Cut out dead wood and about one quarter of the poorly placed living branches, and use them for firewood, cleaning up the prunings under the tree. (Remove other such poorly placed living branches during the next two or three years.) Cultivate the area around the tree out to 2 or 3 feet past its branch spread.

Early the next spring, and before any buds show green, put a dormant oil spray on the tree, and band the trunk with Tanglefoot and with burlap. Now spread 10 to 20 pounds of blood meal around the cultivated area and rake it in. When the weather warms up, spread a 2-inch mulch of compost over this area, and on top of this spread four inches or more of straw. If the tree wants to bear fruit, this treatment will give it the chance it needs.

The sort of tree we're talking about is apt to be an old standard-sized one, but even though it is a dwarf orchard you are interested in, the old standard tree can do you a good turn by providing needed cross-pollination.

• If nematodes are a problem for you, marigolds may help to control them. Place the marigolds 3 feet apart throughout your fruit planting site. The effect they exert is through a root diffusate that repels or kills certain nematodes. It takes effect the year *following* the planting, and lasts for about two more years. Either the tall African or the low French marigolds can be used.

• Peach and nectarine leaves are not for eating, and neither are cherry leaves and twigs. They all contain poison. Children playing at tea-party and making peach-leaf tea, for example, have been affected.

• To space out the ripening of harvested

pears, you can store some of them in a refrigerator set to run cold—about 30° F. This will hold the pears in the unripe stage for up to a month, depending on the variety. Take them out and ripen them at room temperature as you need them.

• Some sweet cherries may crack if there is too much rain near harvest time. The rain causes this by filling the depression in the stem end of the fruits. A way to reduce this damage is to gently shake the tree, spilling the rain from the cherries.

IF TREES FAIL TO BEAR

A fruit tree is a complicated organism, so there are a good many factors that influence its performance. If it should happen that your trees do not bear fruit, or as much fruit as they should, here are some of the things to check, each one followed by what to do, if practical to do so.

Age

Dwarf trees are early bearers, but do need a little time to establish themselves. Although some trees are precocious and will start fruiting quickly, even the year they are planted, here is a general timetable for the age at which a dwarf tree will begin to bear fruit. The age is calculated from the year it is planted.

Apple	1 to 3 years
Pear	3 to 4 years
Peach and Nectarine	1 to 2 years
Plum	2 to 4 years

Sour Cherry	2 to 3 years
Sweet Cherry	3 to 5 years
Apricot	1 to 3 years

Poor Pollination

Check Chapter 4 to see if an appropriate cross-pollinating variety is present, if needed, in your or a neighbor's garden. Either a dwarf or a standard tree will serve the purpose. If there is none, plant the variety needed. It does sometimes happen that even when the right variety for cross-pollination is present, the blossoming season is too wet for the bees to work, or too cold; they stay home if the temperature is below 60° F. Nothing can be done about this, plainly. Nor is it practical for most home gardeners to install a hive of bees to insure pollination.

Insufficient Thinning

If you allowed your tree to bear too many fruits last year, you may get no fruit this year. The remedy is proper thinning, as covered in Chapter 3. Some trees are biennial bearers by nature, but of those we covered, Lodi apple is most apt to be, and hard thinning can correct it there.

Insect or Disease Damage

An invasion of pests may destroy fruit before it can ripen. If this happens when fruits are quite small, the gardener may not realize it and will later be baffled by the lack of a crop. The remedies are: frequent personal attention to the planting, recognizing what pests and pest damage look like, and use of preventives.

Root Competition

If other trees or shrubs compete strongly with dwarf fruit trees for water and nutrients, the dwarf trees will suffer, and may show it by failing to bear fruit. The best remedy is prevention—selecting a site that avoids such competition. Next best: Dig a trench two to four feet deep between the dwarf planting and the competing one, line one side of the trench with galvanized sheet metal, and refill the trench.

Crowded Planting

If you plant dwarf trees closer to each other than the 10-foot spacing recommended in Chapter 2, they are likely to grow leggy and fail to bear well. Respace them by transplanting some elsewhere if they are not too old to be dug up with a bushel-sized ball of earth; or just cut down the excess trees for the sake of the others.

Too Little Sunlight

This is usually caused by nearby trees or buildings shading dwarf trees. Change the site, or remove the cause of the shading if possible. Failure to keep a tree's interior open to sunlight by pruning as needed is also a cause of poor fruiting.

Poor Health

An unhealthy tree has enough to do keeping itself alive without spending energy making fruit. Remember that it takes about 25 leaves to make one apple, so scanty leafing—often a symptom of poor health—reduces production. Remedies are: proper feeding, sanitation, and pest control, as covered in Chapter 3.

Not Enough Winter Chilling

This is most apt to be the case for gardeners in such mild climates as southern California and in the South and Southwest within 100 to 200 miles of the Gulf of Mexico. The cure is to choose varieties that need less winter cold to break their dormancy. Also, do some local investigating before you make a final choice, because within every climate belt there exists many local variations, some in favor of good crops, some against.

Too Cold a Winter

Winter cold that is too cold can cause a crop failure by injuring blossom buds even though the trees can live through it. Variety and maturity of the trees of susceptible species makes a difference in the degree of blossom damage from cold, but the general rule is that peach buds can be hurt by -10° F. to 15° F., sweet cherries by -20° F., and less-hardy pears by -25° F., according to the New York experiment station at Geneva. Hardy apples, pears, plums, and sour cherries are seldom hurt.

Late Frost

If frost comes late in spring, when blossom buds are starting to grow or when flowers have opened, they may be killed even though it is not immediately apparent. If they are killed, the pistil (the small central tube in the flower, the female element that receives the pollen) will blacken and the blossom will presently drop. Since the flower is the precursor to the fruit, when you have no flower you get no fruit. See Chapter 3 for frost-preventive measures.

Excessive Upright Growth

If trees grow more upright than they should for good

fruiting, a small crop or no crop may result. The fruiting branch is ordinarily the horizontally-inclined one. If the tree fruits at all, this problem may not arise, for the fruit itself weighs the branches down toward the horizontal and they more or less stay that way from then on. Tying branches down or using spreaders, as explained previously, is a way to help fruiting.

Overpruning

Pruning a fruit tree too heavily in the dormant season can cause it to spend its energy replacing lost wood instead of growing fruit. And there is another overpruning danger—removing too much fruit-bearing wood. This wood is in the form of spurs on the fruit trees, covered here, except peaches and nectarines, which bear fruit on the branch-end wood that grew the year before. You can see that if you prune off most or all of this new wood, or a good many spurs on the other trees, the crop will be lost. A good pruning rule is: When in doubt, don't prune.

Pollution

Like people, trees breathe, and if the air they breathe is impure, the trees cannot bear normal crops, or sometimes any crops. The pollution may be caused by automobile exhausts if your planting is exposed to these fumes. If the cause is from factory wastes, it would seem high time and a good opportunity to start doing something about it. The alternative is for you to move, but this isn't a very public-spirited solution.

TIPS TO INDUCE FRUITING

To make a tree fruit earlier, or to induce fruiting in a laggard tree, it is sometimes girdled, although this can be considered an emergency measure. Girdling also dwarfs the tree somewhat, even in the case of a standard-sized tree.

The time to do such girdling is three to six weeks after the tree is in full bloom. To girdle a tree, a knife or saw is drawn completely around the trunk a few inches below the lowest branch, making a cut through the bark. This is also called "scoring." The depth of the cut is not critical, and although a cut of this kind is a shock to a tree, it will not, as some gardeners may fear, kill the tree. A more severe form of girdling, called "ringing," is to remove a strip of bark a quarter-inch wide all the way around the trunk; or to remove such a strip halfway around the trunk and remove another one on the opposite side but an inch or so lower or higher on the trunk. Then turn the strips upside down and replace them, fastening them in place with a few brads and a strip of tape. (Do not, of course, turn the strips inside out when replacing them.)

INDUCING FRUITING

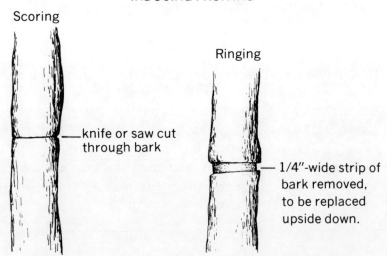

Scoring

knife or saw cut through bark

Ringing

1/4"-wide strip of bark removed, to be replaced upside down.

Root-pruning is another way to induce fruiting. To do this, dig a narrow trench all around the tree. This trench should be one to two feet deep, and a foot or so closer to the trunk than the reach of the farthest branches. Chop off the roots as you dig, then fill the trench in. For a less drastic treatment, dig the trench only halfway around the tree.

FRUIT VARIETIES FOR PROBLEM AREAS

Where winter temperatures drop into the lower ranges, and also where wind increases the effects of cold, extra-hardy varieties of several fruits are more apt to succeed. Other varieties are especially resistant to some diseases, and still others are more tolerant of zonal limitations than most of their species. Here is a selection of some such adaptable varieties. Each, except where noted, is available in dwarf size.

Apples

Honeygold

A development from the Minnesota experiment station, this hardy apple is a Golden Delicious cross with Haralson. The skin is a warm yellow with red dots and a red blush. The flesh is yellowish, crisp, and juicy, reminiscent of its Golden Delicious parentage. It ripens in October.|(Farmer)

Red Baron

Another Minnesota station development, this is also a hybrid, a cross of Golden Delicious and Red Duchess. Colored medium-light red with yellow dots, it ripens in late summer or fall, and is blight-resistant along with being hardy. (Farmer)

Regent

This third hardy hybrid from the Minnesota station is

a Red Delicious and Duchess cross. It is a bright red apple with good flavor, and it has the good point of clinging fast to the tree until thoroughly ripe. It is an exceptionally good keeper. (Farmer)

Anoka

This is an old variety with a reputation for hardiness. Red with yellow stripes, it ripens in August, and for an early apple, it is a good keeper. Although not ranking as a choice dessert apple, it does deserve consideration by those gardeners whose problem is cold winter weather. (Ackerman)

Fireside

This Red Delicious type is not as well colored as Red Delicious, but has crisp, sweet flesh, is very hardy, and keeps well. (Farmer)

Haralson

Ripening in October, this big red well-flavored and tart apple keeps fairly well—till February or so—and is resistant to blight. (Farmer, Gurney, and Interstate)

Starkspur EarliBlaze

This productive tree's good record in resisting damage from scab, mildew, and blotch deserves an added mention here as well as a listing among the good varieties in Chapter 4. (Stark)

Winter Banana

One of the few apples that will produce fruit in a mild climate, Winter Banana is not available in dwarf size smaller than on EM 7 rootstocks, so far as we know. The variety will also bear fruit in colder climates—and indeed originated in Indiana, about 100 years ago—but its chief claim to attention is its low chilling requirement. It acquired its name not for its tropical leanings but because the fruits have a banana-like fragrance. Skin color is a light yellow blushed with pink, and the apples are good keepers. (Miller)

Pears

Kieffer

The famed pomologist U. P. Hedrick cared so little for the Kieffer pear, he seemed to take its existence as almost a personal affront, calling it "the most pretentious cheat in the orchard." and clouting it with a "poor" rating on quality. But Kieffer is a good scout, highly resistant to fire blight, and willing to put up with growing conditions other pears wouldn't tolerate for a minute. Also, a properly ripened Kieffer is well worth eating fresh, and is good enough when canned to pass for Bartlett—which it often has.

We grew a relative of Kieffer's, Le Conte, when we lived on the Mississippi Gulf Coast, where gentler pears gave up the ghost. We found Le Conte a good dessert fruit when wrapped in soft paper and allowed to take its time ripening at room temperature. It made splendid preserves too.

Kieffer will also do well in climates colder than many pears will take. It is one of several hybrids of which the sturdy though low-quality Chinese Sand pear is one parent. In Kieffer's case the other parent was most likely Bartlett, because the original Kieffer tree grew as a seedling in a garden near Philadelphia, where both Bartlett and Chinese Sand pears were being grown. Kieffer's name dates to the Civil War period and came from the man who owned the garden, Peter Kieffer. Zones 4 to 9. (Boatman, Leuthardt, Savage, and Stark)

Moonglow

A U.S. Department of Agriculture development, this agreeably tart eating and cooking pear is resistant to scab and very resistant to blight, and is an unusually good producer. It matures about two weeks ahead of Bartlett, during August, and ripens in another two weeks during indoor storage. Zones 5 to 8. (Ackerman, Boatman, Miller, Southmeadow, and Stark)

Starking Delicious

This variety is exclusive with the Stark Bro's Nurseries, who call it the most disease-resistant pear they have ever found. Like Seckel, the fruits can be ripened on the tree, but they are somewhat fuller flavored if ripened indoors. The pears are large and handsome, as good keepers in cold storage as Magness, and are smooth-fleshed and well flavored. They ripen in September. Zones 5 to 8. (Stark)

Peaches

Early White Giant

Ripening quite early, during the first week in July, this white-fleshed freestone peach is a beautiful fruit, the skin red with white splashes. Quality is good, and severe thinning is recommended—8 inches between young fruits. Early White Giant is particularly resistant to scab and to bacterial spot, and is hardy. Zones 5 to 8. (Stark)

Reliance

The quality of this peach is good, as is the tree's ability to take cold weather. Bred at the New Hampshire experiment station, Reliance has borne fruit after suffering through a winter in which the temperature dropped to -28° F. The dark red fruits are yellow-fleshed and freestone. Zones 5 to 8. (Gurney, Interstate, and Stark)

Note: Although not offered in dwarf size, we should perhaps mention here the exceptionally hardy Presidential Series of peaches bred at the Virginia experiment station and introduced over the past 20 years. Peach trees, as noted in Chapter 7, can be held at a reasonable 10-foot height without much trouble, making a standard peach tree a dwarf in effect. All the Presidential varieties are hybrids, and bear buds that are able to endure late spring frosts much better than most peaches. Four in the series will give an excellent ripening spread, over a period of six weeks. They are those listed below, and the dates given are for Virginia, but the intervals would remain about the same in other peach country.

Harrison

Very new, introduced in 1973, this yellow-fleshed freestone peach with good quality and texture ripens in late July. (Waynesboro)

Madison

Producing an unusually heavy set of buds, this yellow freestone with richly colored and slightly fibrous sweet flesh ripens in mid-August. (N.Y. Co-op and Waynesboro)

Jefferson

Perhaps the most all-around peach of this group, Jefferson has good looks, vigor, large fruits of good dessert quality, and is resistant to brown rot. It will need heavy thinning of fruits, which ripen very late in August. (N.Y. Co-op and Waynesboro)

Tyler

A vigorous, heavy bloomer, ripening its fruits in early September, Tyler's attractive yellow-fleshed peaches are a good size, with very firm, mild flesh; they are fully freestone. One of its parents was Rio Oso Gem, well known for its good fruit. (N.Y. Co-op and Waynesboro)

Plums

Beach Plum

This is a native American plum, *Prunus maritima*, a hardy hedge-like plant that can get 10 feet tall, but usually doesn't, and can be kept pruned low. It is native to the eastern seaboard as far north as Maine, but will adapt itself to some other areas and is at home on poor or sandy soil. Plant two for best pollination. The fruits are small and purple, too tart for eating fresh but good for jams and jelly. (Gurney, Kelly, and Miller)

Cherry Plum

More precisely called the Myrobalan plum (*Prunus cerasifera*), this native of southeastern Asia is often employed as a rootstock for other plums and for apricots, but some improved forms of cherry plums are of dwarf habit, are adapted to cold climates, and are well worth growing for their fruits. The variety Oka (Ackerman and Field) bears sweet black inch-wide fruits in early August in the upper Midwest, and should be grown near European plums for cross-pollination, or near another variety of cherry plum. Two hybrids are Sapalta and Compass (Farmer), which are pollinators for each other and will pollinate Oka.

Idaho Prune

This European type plum has taken colder winters

than others and is possibly as hardy as Damsons. Ripening its heavy load of good-sized blue fruits in August, Idaho is for eating fresh as well as for cooking. (Gurney)

Cherries

Meteor

This cherry is a semi-dwarf, growing to 15 feet tall, though you can keep it lower with pruning. It is an attractive tree and bears good crops of tart, light red cherries. Originated at the Minnesota experiment station it is, as you might expect, especially able to take cold winters. Mainly for cooking and freezing, it ripens in June. Zones 4 to 7. (Boatman, Farmer, Field, Gurney, Interstate, and Stark)

> *Note:* In addition to the usual cherries there are those species for which the chief use is as rootstocks on which to graft peaches, plums, cherries, and apricots. These rootstock cherries include the Mahaleb, Mazzard, Nanking, and Western Sand cherries. However, the fruits of some of these otherwise rootstock cherries are well worth having. You can get Nanking and Western Sand, both at home in rugged-winter climates. In addition, the hybrid bush cherries are also worth considering if you live in a cold climate, for they too are quite hardy and produce lots of good fruit.

Nanking Cherry

Very hardy and of several types, including hybrids, Nanking, *Prunus tomentosa*, grows into a shrubby dwarf tree 6 to 10 feet tall, and has small, bright red little cherries, tart and juicy. They ripen with sour cherries, and you'll need a sour cherry or one of the other Nanking types nearby for cross-pollination. Gurney has the widest selection, and two other houses, Boatman and N.Y. Co-op, carry Nanking.

Western Sand Cherry

Native to the Sand Hills area of Nebraska, this little sweet cherry, *Prunus besseyi*, was prized by the Dakota Indians and nearby tribes. The cherries grow wild on bushes that seldom get taller than 30 inches, but may grow twice that tall in cultivation. The purplish-black fruits average half an inch wide. The Indians ate them fresh in season and cooked them. They also sun-dried them for winter food. You can do the same thing in your oven: Wash the cherries, cut them in halves and remove the seeds. Put them in a bowl and pour boiling water over them. Drain after 15 minutes, place them on a cooky sheet with cut sides up, and put them in a 130° F. oven. After two or three hours increase temperature to 165° F. and continue drying until the cherries feel almost as dry as a prune. Then lower the temperature to 130° F. for a final three hours or so. The total drying time should be about ten hours, but the test is that the fruit will feel like soft leather when done. (Boatman, Gurney, Kelly, and Mellinger)

Bush Cherries

Hybrid bush cherries, grafted to rootstocks of native plum, give good crops of fair-sized fruits, are exceptionally hardy, and are not subject to some cherry troubles. Also, they grow dense enough foliage to screen their fruit from birds. Keep an eye out for possible shoots growing from the plum rootstock; these should be pruned off when they arise.

Varieties among the bush cherries include Sioux, a nearly black sweet cherry with greenish flesh that ripens late in July (Ackerman); White Gold, a mild-flavored yellow cherry (Ackerman); South Dakota Ruby (Field), and Brooks (Field and Gurney) both being dark red; and Hansen's Improved, a purple-fruited variety that grows 4 to 5 feet tall (Field, Gurney, Mellinger, and Miller).

Apricots

Moongold

A University of Minnesota development, this extra-hardy hybrid apricot tree can take -25° F. without harm. The medium-sized yellow fruits ripen in July, are free-stone and good quality. Moongold needs a pollinator nearby, such as Sungold. Zones 5 to 8. (Miller)

Sungold

This is the companion of Moongold, with the same breeding and same general characteristics, but growing in a slightly more upright form, and ripening its fruit a week later, in late July. Use another apricot, such as Moongold, for a pollinator. Zones 5 to 8. (Miller)

9

The Fruit Gardener's Calendar

Here is a month-by-month reminder of things to do for your dwarf-tree orchard. When the timing is given by zones, they are the zones shown on the Plant Hardiness Zone Map. Keep in mind that zones are 300 or 400 miles wide in places, so the timing here is a general guide. Check it against your local weather pattern. Remember also that if you live near a zone's boundary, your climate will be a mix of that in your own zone and that in the zone just next to it.

References

Fertilizing, frost, watering, mulching, and thinning: (*see Chapter 3*).

Pruning and pest control: (*see Chapters 3, 4, and 8*).

Container-planting: (*see Chapter 5*).

Espaliers: (*see Chapter 6*).

Suppliers: (*see Chapter 10*).

JANUARY

Zones 7-9

Give trees their annual dormant pruning now if not done last month.

Give trees their annual fertilizing now if not done last month.

Plant bare-root trees whenever soil can be worked.

Repot container trees as needed.

Apply dormant oil spray before any growth starts, when temperature is above 50° F.

Scrape and burn loose bark from apple trees, scrub trunks and limbs with soapy water, and band trunks with burlap and with Tanglefoot.

Apply sulfur spray for prevention of apple scab and peach leaf-curl, if necessary.

General

Inspect branches for cocoons and insect egg clusters, and destroy them. Continue to look for web caterpillar eggs (*see November calendar*).

It is now getting late to order nursery stock for spring delivery.

Prune off any storm-damaged wood in trees cleanly, now and later in the winter.

PLANT HARDINESS ZONE MAP

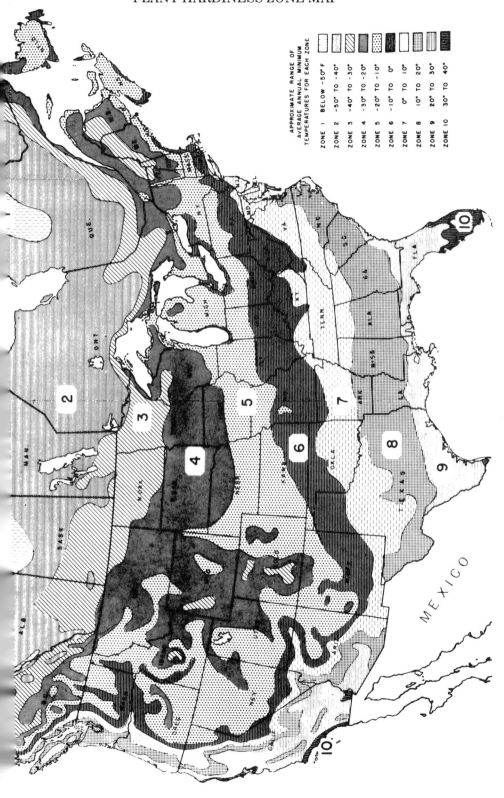

APPROXIMATE RANGE OF
AVERAGE ANNUAL MINIMUM
TEMPERATURES FOR EACH ZONE

ZONE 1 BELOW -50°F
ZONE 2 -50° TO -40°
ZONE 3 -40° TO -30°
ZONE 4 -30° TO -20°
ZONE 5 -20° TO -10°
ZONE 6 -10° TO 0°
ZONE 7 0° TO 10°
ZONE 8 10° TO 20°
ZONE 9 20° TO 30°
ZONE 10 30° TO 40°

FEBRUARY

Zones 4-6

Give annual dormant pruning to apple, pear, plum, and cherry trees.

Give trees their annual fertilizing.

Repot container trees as needed.

Apply dormant oil spray before any growth starts, when temperature is above 50° F.

Apply sulfur spray for prevention of apple scab and peach leaf-curl, if necessary.

Zones 7-9

Prune all trees not yet pruned.

Plant bare-root trees if soil can be worked.

Give annual fertilizing to any trees not yet taken care of.

In dry areas, water and mulch if needed.

Finish scraping and banding apple trees.

General

Nursery stock ordered now for spring delivery may already be sold out.

MARCH

Zones 4-6

Give annual dormant pruning to any trees not yet pruned.

Last chance to apply dormant oil spray.

Give annual fertilizing to any trees not yet taken care of.

Scrape and burn loose bark from apple trees, scrub

trunks and limbs with soapy water, and band trunks with burlap and Tanglefoot.

Apply sulfur spray if needed, if not done last month.

Plant bare-root trees when soil can be worked.

Zones 7-9

Last chance to plant bare-root trees.

Give annual fertilizing to any trees not yet fertilized.

General

Control web caterpillars by clipping off twig ends with the web and burning it. Do this at *sundown*, after caterpillars have returned to the web for the night.

Start checking for peach borers.

APRIL

Zones 4-6

In colder areas, finish setting out bare-root trees; finish annual dormant pruning; finish annual fertilizing.

In warmer areas, water newly planted trees if needed; spread mulch.

Zones 7-9

In dry areas, water deeply if needed; spread mulch.

General

Take preventive measures against borers.

If brown rot has been a problem, start sulfur sprays on each fruit (peach, nectarine, plum, cherry, apricot) *before* they begin to ripen.

Keep after web caterpillars (*see March calendar*).

MAY

Zones 4-6

Replenish mulch as needed, to hold moisture in soil.

Zones 7-9

In dry areas, water deeply when needed; keep mulch at proper depth.

General

Keep an eye on possible fungus attacks, especially if weather is wet. Peaches and plums are vulnerable.

Keep dropped fruit cleaned up and buried.

Keep weeds down.

Water newly planted trees as needed.

Keep after web caterpillars now and later (*see March calendar*).

Begin taking recommended measures, according to your season, against aphids, codling moths, and scale.

JUNE

Zones 7-9

Thin peaches, nectarines, apricots.

Whitewash trunks of young trees.

In dry areas, water as needed; mulch.

General

Keep dropped fruit raked up and buried.

Keep weeds down.

Remove watersprouts.

Seed cover crop where you intend to plant trees next spring.

Water newly planted trees if needed.

Check for borer damage.

Prune out any winter-killed dead branches.

Begin summer pruning of espaliers.

JULY

Zones 4-6

Thin developing fruits as needed.

Whitewash trunks of young trees.

Zones 7-9

Thin apples, pears, plums.

General

Water, and replenish mulch, as needed.

Keep weeds down.

Hang maggot-fly traps in apple and pear trees.

Continue to summer-prune espaliers.

AUGUST

General

This month and next, keep gathering all dropped apples, to prevent any maggots in them from over-wintering in the soil.

Inspect under mulches for possible pests.

If you want your soil tested for acidity, this is the time to have it done. If lime is needed, add it during the next two months.

This month, *finish* summer-pruning of espaliers.

SEPTEMBER

General

If you have not planted a cover crop to be turned under where new trees are to go next spring, spread a mulch on the area now, and let it remain.

Spread lime if a need is indicated by a soil test. If test should indicate your soil not acid enough—seldom the case—dig in old sawdust, or peat moss, instead of spreading lime.

Make preparations for storing surplus apples and pears this winter in a cool room or basement. In addition, an old spare refrigerator makes a good cold-storage unit.

Take a gift basket of your fruit to a friend, a neighbor, a shut-in.

Send for nursery catalogs.

OCTOBER

Zones 4-5

Plant dormant cherry trees early this month in northern areas, later this month in warmer ones.

General

Rake up and bury dropped fruits. Clean out debris, fallen leaves, and weeds. Burn plum leaves. Burn all prunings. Remove and burn any dried peaches and nectarines hanging on trees.

Spread lime if not yet done and a need is indicated by a soil test(*see September calendar*).

Rake mulch 6 to 12 inches away from trunks, and protect trunks from animal damage with hardware cloth cylinders. Add fresh mulch as needed, anchoring it with rocks, etc., in winter-windy areas.

Make sure stakes offer good support for trees in winter storms.

From now on, check stored fruits frequently for any spoilage, and remove any affected fruits at once.

Send for nursery catalogs.

Order nursery stock for spring delivery.

NOVEMBER

Zones 6-7

Plant dormant cherry trees this month. North Star cherry can be planted in Zone 8 this month or next.

General

Complete garden sanitation chores that were begun in October.

Remove and burn any egg masses of web caterpillar on trees (gray lumps with gritty surfaces).

Finish protecting trunks from animals, as in October. Add fresh mulch as needed. In colder areas set windbreaks, snow fences.

Set new support stakes for trees as needed.

Check plum and cherry branches for black knot, and cut out any infected places.

Send for nursery catalogs.

Order nursery stock for spring delivery.

DECEMBER

Zones 4-6

Last chance to complete any sanitation and tree-protection chores that were not finished in October and November.

Zones 7-9

In warmer areas apply dormant oil spray when temperature is 50° F. or higher, and before any new growth starts. Give trees their annual fertilizing. Give annual dormant pruning.

Plant bare-root trees whenever soil can be worked.

In colder areas, repot container trees now, as needed.

General

Continue to look for web caterpillar eggs (*see November calendar*).

Getting late to send for nursery catalogs.

Order nursery stock for spring delivery, if you have not yet done so.

Buy a diary to keep next year's garden record in.

Set up bird feeders for the winter.

Growing little Lady apples? Decorate the Christmas tree and wreaths with some of them.

10

Where To to Find What You Need

MAIL ORDER NURSERIES

Ackerman Nurseries,
Bridgman, Michigan, 49106.
This northern nursery has some interesting bush cherries among its dwarf trees, mentioned in Chapter 8.

Armstrong Nurseries,
Ontario California, 91761.
Although mostly an ornamentals house and notably strong in rose breeding, Armstrong pioneered with the improved forms of genetic dwarf peaches and nectarines.

Boatman's Nursery & Seed Company,
Bainbridge, Ohio, 45612.
Specializing in serving the Michigan-Ohio-Tennessee region, this nursery's helpful catalog offers a selection of well-known varieties in dwarf sizes, as well as some bush cherries.

Burgess Seed and Plant Company,
Galesburg, Michigan, 49053.

The handsome catalog of this northern house lists a representative selection of good varieties in dwarfs.

W. Atlee Burpee Company,
Philadelphia, Pennsylvania, 19132;
Clinton, Iowa, 52732; and Riverside, California, 92502.
This long-established seed house with an international trade and one of the best catalogs in the business, handles a group of dependable dwarf varieties of fruit trees, including some dwarfs that are not easily available elsewhere.

Farmer Seed and Nursery Company,
Faribault, Minnesota, 55021.
Stressing hardy varieties for northern winters, and working closely with their state experiment station, Farmer carries an interesting group of dwarf apples, and a few other fruits in dwarf-size trees.

Henry Field Seed & Nursery Company,
Shenandoah, Iowa, 51601.
The helpful and good-sized catalog carries an adequate selection of dwarf fruit trees, as well as several bush cherries.

Gurney Seed & Nursery Company,
Yankton, South Dakota, 57078.
As with some of the other northern houses, Gurney takes an adventurous approach to home fruit growing, offering in its big-page catalog a large selection of good native fruits in bush or hedge-height form; they also list the more usual dwarf fruit trees.

H. G. Hastings Company,
Box 4088, Atlanta, Georgia, 30302.
Featuring stempiece grafts with their dwarf apples, this southern house carries a few other dwarf fruit trees, including one of the seldom available species dwarf peaches, Mandarin.

Interstate Nurseries,
Hamburg, Iowa, 51640.
This is one of the largest nurseries in the country.
Their attractive catalog offers a good selection of dwarf
fruit trees, mainly of the well-known varieties, including
some not found elsewhere.

Kelly Bros. Nurseries,
Dansville, New York, 14437.
Some unusual items, such as a native plum and a cherry,
and a few old apple varieties, are included among a
representative listing of dwarf fruit trees in their well done
catalog.

Henry Leuthardt Nurseries,
East Moriches, Long Island, New York, 11940.
This nursery specializes in dwarf fruit trees, and the
listing includes a number of rare and choice varieties. The
neat catalog well deserves the name handbook, for
more than half its pages are devoted to fruit culture
and allied topics. Espaliered trees are a specialty here.
There is a 25¢ charge for the catalog.

Mellinger's,
2310 West South Range Road, North Lima, Ohio, 44452.
A few dwarf fruit trees are among the vast number of
items carried by this house, which lists all sorts of horticultural things, including East Malling rootstocks.

J. E. Miller Nurseries,
Canandaigua, New York, 14424.
A nice choice of dwarf fruits, except apples. (Apple trees
are offered in semi-dwarf size only, on EM 7 rootstocks.
But they include a number of intriguing old varieties
along with a very good assortment of others; among them
is Winter Banana, a variety that will fruit in mild
climates.)

New York State Fruit Testing Cooperative Association,
Geneva, New York, 14456.

This organization in conjunction with the New York
State Agricultural Experiment Station at Geneva has
been testing new fruits—mainly those developed by the
New York station—since 1918, and has 5000 members
throughout the United States and many foreign countries. Members pay dues of $4 a year, which brings them
the annual catalog from which they may order any of the
trees and plants listed for trial in their own areas. The
$4 counts as a credit toward any such purchase. A wide
choice of dwarfing rootstocks is offered in the tree listings,
and the rootstocks themselves are also available for the
hobbyist gardener. Anyone interested in Chapter 7 will
find the N.Y. Co-op catalog a good reference book.

Savage Farms Nursery,
P.O. Box 125, McMinnville, Tennessee, 37110.
A small nursery, Savage includes a few dwarf fruit trees in
their brief and nicely handled catalog.

Southmeadow Fruit Gardens,
2363 Tilbury Place, Birmingham, Michigan, 48009.
The conveniently pocket-sized catalog lists, as it states,
"choice and unusual fruit varieties for the connoisseur
and home gardener." The varieties are those selected
by a serious avocational fruit grower of long experience,
Mr. Robert A. Nitschke. The number of apple varieties
is especially large and noteworthy. Again—the readers
who find particular interest in Chapter 7 will find the
Southmeadow catalog a permanent reference. The catalog
costs $1; a price list is available without charge.

Stark Bro's Nurseries,
Louisiana, Missouri, 63353.
This large nursery with a world-wide trade and with
nearly 160 years of experience behind it under the same
family management is in a class by itself in many
respects. It stresses exclusive varieties, of which it has
more than any other nursery, or even all others put
together. Stark introduced the famous Delicious apples,

along with many other leading varieties of fruits, and apples are its strongest line today. The house is also strong in dwarf pears and peaches. Research gets a considerable part of the budget at Stark, and the lavishly illustrated catalog reflects this and has a good deal of basic information in it.

Waynesboro Nurseries,
Waynesboro, Virginia, 22980.
This good-sized southern nursery works closely with the Virginia experiment station, and offers a listing of dwarf trees, strongest in apples.

PEST CONTROLS

Bacillus thuringiensis. This is a biological control of certain caterpillars and worms, and is harmless to other creatures. It is now becoming generally available at local garden supply centers. Manufactured by several firms, it is sold under such trade names as Thuricide, Dipel, and Biotrol.

Bio-Dynamic Spray. This non-chemical fruit tree spray is a general insecticide; the active ingredients are ryania, rotenone, and pyrethum. A clay base is used and is thought to be beneficial to tree health. The spray may be purchased from Peter A. Escher, Three-Fold Farm, Spring Valley, New York, 10977.

Other organic sprays. Two houses handle these: Hopkins Agricultural Chemical Company, Box 584, Madison, Wisconsin, 53701; and Natural Development Company, Bainbridge, Pennsylvania, 17502.

Perma-Guard. This is a trade name for an insecticide mixture consisting largely of a natural product, diatomaceous earth—which is primarily made up of cell walls of microscopic algae from past eons. The diatomaceous earth kills certain insects by cutting them when they move over it, in a kind of broken-glass action. We include this product here as a possibility about which little is known, but which seems to offer something to those gardeners who will experiment with it. It should not be breathed, but otherwise seems to be non-toxic to persons. It is applied as a dust to damp foliage, either weekly or when target insects are present. It has shown effectiveness against such varied pests as ants, aphids, codling moths, earwigs, mites, and twig borers.

At present it is mainly sold direct from the manufacturer: Perma-Guard Division, Bower Industires, Inc., P.O. Box 21024, Phoenix, Arizona, 85036. A pound sells for $2.95, five pounds for $8. Ask for "Perma-Guard Garden & Plant Insecticide." George W. Park Seed Company, P.O. Box 31, Greenwood, South Carolina, 29646. also handles it in the one-pound size, and in 8-ounce duster cans.

Bug Bait. This is a spray that attracts some helpful insects to your garden, to prey on harmful ones. Order from World Garden Products, World Building, East Norwalk, Connecticut, 06855.

Netting. Although birds destroy many harmful insects, when a fruit crop ripens, the birds may also destroy much of it. A practical way for a home fruit gardener to protect his trees at this time is with nylon mesh netting sold for this purpose. It is now becoming available at many local garden centers. If you cannot find it in your vicinity, here are four sources: Animal Repellents, P.O. Box 168, Griffin, Georgia, 30223; Apex Mills, Inc., 49 West 37th Street, New York, New York, 10018; Conwed Corporation, 332 Minnesota Street, St. Paul, Minnesota, 55101; Frank Coviello, 1300 83rd Street, North Bergen, New Jersey, 07047.

Ryania. If you cannot find this insecticide locally, it can be ordered from Hopkins, previously mentioned, or from

S. B. Penick & Company, 100 Church Street, New York, New York, 10007.

Tanglefoot. In the forms of a spray, a syrupy liquid, and a flypaper, this product to trap insects is available from some seed houses and from The Tanglefoot Company, 314 Straight Avenue S.W., Grand Rapids, Michigan, 49500.

Soil tests. An organic house is Biochemical Research Laboratory, Threefold Farms, Spring Valley, New York, 10977. For local or regional laboratories, see your county agent.

Fruit storage. Here are two good government bulletins describing methods of storing fruit. Order them from: Superintendent of Documents, U.S. Government Printing Office, Washington, D.C., 20402. Make payment in coins. "Storing Vegetables and Fruits in Basements, Cellars, Outbuildings, and Pits" 15¢. "Storing Perishable Foods in the Home" 10¢.

Canning. Two informative government bulletins on canning, available from the same source as the fruit storage bulletins, are: "Home Canning of Fruits and Vegetables" 20¢; "How to make Jellies, Jams, and Preserves at Home" 20¢. An excellent and comprehensive handbook on canning fruits is "Kerr Home Canning Book," Kerr Glass Manufacturing Corporation, Sand Springs, Oklahoma, 74063, 35¢.

STATE AND COUNTY INFORMATION SOURCES

County agent. The county agricultural agent, or farm advisor, is usually at the county seat. Look in your telephone directory under your county office listings. Although chronically overloaded with work, the county agent is an excellent source of information on fruit-garden matters, and can usually supply government bulletins on various aspects of it.

State Department of Agriculture. Found in the capital city of your state, the state department of agriculture supplies some published fruit-gardening information in leaflet, bulletin, and booklet forms, usually free. Write for titles.

State Agricultural Experiment Station and State Extension Service. The State Experiment Station can inform you as to which fruits are suited to your area. The Extension Service has information on a broad range of horticultural activities. Usually both offices are in the same place; if the State Extension Service is at a different location, that address is listed in the right-hand column. When writing either office, address your requests to "The Director."

State	State Agricultural Experiment Station	State Extension Service
Alabama	Auburn, 36830	same
Alaska	College, 99730	same
Arizona	Tucson, 85721	same
Arkansas	Fayetteville, 72701	P.O. Box 391 Little Rock, 72203
California	Berkeley, 94720	same
Colorado	Fort Collins, 80521	same
Connecticut	New Haven, 06504	
	Storrs, 06268 (Agricultural College)	
Delaware	Newark, 19711	same
Florida	Gainesville, 32603	same
Georgia	Experiment, 30212 (Main Station) Tifton, 31794 (Coastal Plains Station)	Athens, 30601
Hawaii	Honolulu, 96822	same
Idaho	Moscow, 83843	same
Illinois	Urbana, 61801	same

State	State Agricultural Experiment Station	State Extension Service
Indiana	Lafayette, 47907	same
Iowa	Ames, 50010	same
Kansas	Manhattan, 66504	same
Kentucky	Lexington, 40506	same
Louisiana	Baton Rouge, 70803	same
Maine	Orono, 04473	same
Maryland	College Park, 20740	same
Massachusetts	Amherst, 01003	same
Michigan	East Lansing, 48823	same
Minnesota	St. Paul, 55101	same
Mississippi	State College, 39762	same
Missouri	Columbia, 65202 (Main Station) Mountain Grove, 65711 (Fruit Station)	same
Montana	Bozeman, 59715	same
Nebraska	Lincoln, 68503	same
Nevada	Reno, 89507	same
New Hampshire	Durham, 03824	same
New Jersey	New Brunswick, 08900	same
New Mexico	University Park, 88070	same
New York	Geneva, 14456 (State Station) Ithaca, 14850 (Cornell Station)	same
North Carolina	Raleigh, 27607	same
North Dakota	Fargo, 58103	same
Ohio	Wooster, 44691	Columbus, 43210
Oklahoma	Stillwater, 74075	same
Oregon	Corvallis, 97331	same
Pennsylvania	University Park, 16802	same
Rhode Island	Kingston, 02881	same
South Carolina	Clemson, 29631	same
South Dakota	Brookings, 57007	same
Tennessee	Knoxville, 37901	same
Texas	College Station, 77843	same
Utah	Logan, 84321	same
Vermont	Burlington, 05401	same

State	State Agricultural Experiment Station	State Extension Service
Virginia	Blacksburg, 24061 (Main Station) Norfolk, 23501 (Truck Station	same
Washington	Pullman, 99163	same
West Virginia	Morgantown, 26506	same
Wisconsin	Madison, 53706	same
Wyoming	Laramie, 82701	same

GLOSSARY

AXIL   The upper angle at the point where a branch joins another branch or joins the trunk.

BIOLOGICAL CONTROL   The control of a pest by another organism rather than by chemical, mechanical, or other means.

BLOSSOM END   The bottom of a fruit—the end opposite from the stem end.

BUD   The beginning stage of a shoot, a leaf, or a flower.

BUDDING   A method of grafting, in which a leaf bud of one variety of fruit is fastened to and grows into part of another variety. In this way, a tree's main trunk and roots may be of one variety, and the fruit-bearing top will be grown from a bud grafted on the other.

CALLUS   The protective new tissue that forms over a wound on a tree, such as over a pruning cut.

CAMBIUM   A very thin living layer just under the outer bark. By cellular division, the cambium makes the tree grow in girth of trunk and limbs.

CHILLING REQUIREMENT   A fruit tree's need for a certain number of hours of cold weather each winter. The reason the tree needs this cold weather is to put an end to the dormant (resting) state it passes into after the growing season ends.

Lacking proper chilling, a tree will leaf out late and poorly, its blossoms will be sparse, and its general health will decline. A temperature of 45° F. is often cold enough for the purpose. The number of hours it is needed varies with the kind of fruit and the variety, but 500 hours is a rough average. A tree with a high chilling requirement may need 750 or more hours of cold weather, whereas a tree with a low chilling requirement might need only 300 hours of temperatures of about 55° F. To some extent, fog can substitute for cool temperatures in filling a tree's chilling requirement.

CLARK DWARF   An apple tree dwarfed by using a stempiece (see STEMPIECE) from a Clark Dwarf apple tree, named for the man who brought it to horticultural attention.

CLINGSTONE   A drupe (stone fruit) character in which the seed adheres to the flesh. Opposite of freestone.

CLONE   See Cutting.

COVER CROP   A temporary planting, as of a grass or clover, to protect soil from erosion, and often intended to be spaded under for the benefit of a future planting. This spading under is called green-manuring.

CROSS   An abbreviation for cross-pollinating, also used as a noun to denote the offspring. To cross-pollinate is to place the pollen (male element) of one flower on the pistil (female receptacle) of another, whether done by humans, insects, or such other means as gravity or wind.

CUTTING   A living piece of half-hard wood cut from a plant for the purpose of sprouting it into a complete separate plant. Slip and clone are synonyms for cutting.

DRUPE   Technical word for a stone fruit such as peach, plum, cherry, or apricot.

EAST MALLING   The research station in Kent, England, responsible for standardizing the rootstocks most used for dwarfing apple trees. The initials "EM" or "M" followed by a number are employed to designate these various rootstocks.

ESPALIER   A tree trained to grow almost flat, as against a wall, and in one of several patterns such as a single-U, double-U, gridiron, etc.

FRAMEWORK BRANCH   One of the main branches of a tree, forming a part of the tree's basic shape.

FREESTONE   A drupe (stone fruit) character in which the seed is not attached to the flesh. Opposite of clingstone.

FORCING   Throwing strength into one part of a plant, as a bud, by depriving some farther-out growth of sap, often done simply by removing all or part of the farther-out growth.

GENETIC DWARF   A natural dwarf tree, as contrasted with one dwarfed through an outside influence, such as by grafting.

GENUS   This term (plural: genera) is the major subdivision of a family of fruits. The pear genus, for instance, is *Pyrus* (always capitalized, and in italics). This genus is a member of the rose family. The *Pyrus* genus is made up of about 20 different species. Most of our fruit-bearing pears belong to the *communis* species (meaning common, familiar), so are referred to as *Pyrus communis.*

To show which particular pear is being talked about, the variety name is added, like this: *Pyrus communis bart-lett*, referring to the Bartlett pear. The Bartlett pear is so well known that you wouldn't ordinarily bother to spell out its full botanical name in this way, but for lesser-known fruits it helps keep things straight.

GIRDLING   The making of any encircling cut or restriction around the trunk of a tree, resulting in a restriction of free movement of nutrients and other substances to and from the roots. Bark nibblers such as mice and deer may girdle a tree, or a vine may do so through a kind of strangulation. However, girdling is also done deliberately by gardeners at times, usually to induce fruiting.

GRAFTING   The physical joining of one living plant tissue to another, with the object of making them grow together into a single plant. See Scion and Stock.

GRAFT UNION   The point at which a graft is attached to a plant.

GREEN-MANURING   Improving structure and richness of soil by spading under a cover crop (see COVER CROP).

GROUND COLOR   A fruit's basic color, often blushed or striped with reddish tints from exposure to sun.

HALF-HARD   Said of wood that has partly matured, being neither succulent nor woody. At this stage such wood is useful for making cuttings.

HEADING BACK   A pruning term meaning to shorten a branch or the central stem of a tree.

HYBRID   The offspring of unlike parents, usually parents of the same species but different varieties.

INDIGENOUS   Native, not brought in from elsewhere. Opposite of introduced.

INTERSTOCK   See Stempiece.

INTRODUCED   See Indigenous. "Introduced" is also used to refer to the original marketing of a new fruit variety.

LATERAL   A branch growing in a somewhat horizontal position, usually growing out from a fairly vertical trunk.

MULCH   A covering, as of straw, laid on the soil to benefit plants by retaining more soil moisture, keeping roots cooler in summer, etc.

pH   When followed by a number, this is a measure of acidity in soil. A soil measuring pH 7.0 is neutral; the lower the number, the more acid the soil, and the higher the number, the more alkaline.

PINCHING   Pruning a shoot, bud, etc., by cutting it off with the thumbnail pressed against a finger.

PISTIL   That part of a flower that contains the ovary and produces the fruit. Thus, the female part. See Pollination.

POLLINATION   The successful transfer of pollen, a flower's male element, to the pistil, a flower's female organ.

POME   Technical word for the fruit of an apple, pear, and related species. The word comes from the Latin *poma*, for fruit, and from it is also derived the word for the science that deals with fruits, pomology.

RESISTANT   Said of a plant that is less susceptible to some diseases than some other plants of its kind.

RIPENESS   The stage at which a fruit is ready to be eaten. Terms used to describe the degree of ripeness are "hard," meaning flesh that resists pressure of the fingers; "firm," a flesh that gives slightly to pressure; and "soft," a flesh that can be pressed in. The term "mature" is used for a fruit that either is ripe or that will ripen after being picked, as with most pears.

ROOTSTOCK   See Stock.

RUSSET   A brownish coloring in the skin, often found in certain apples.

SAP   The juice that transports nutrients within the plant body.

SCION   A piece of living wood from one tree intended to be grafted onto another tree. The word "scion" can mean the eventual fruit-bearing top part of a tree that is developed with the aid of grafting. A scion may be either a twig with buds, or a single bud.

SEEDLING   A tree that grew from a seed, whether planted by man or otherwise. Such reproduction is called sexual, contrasting with vegetative reproduction by rooting a cutting.

SELF-FRUITFUL   Ability to produce fruit without needing pollen from another plant.

SELF-STERILE   Unable to produce fruit without the assistance of pollen from another plant. Also called "self-unfruitful."

SEMI-DWARF   A fruit tree larger than a dwarf tree and smaller than a standard tree of its species.

SHOOT   New woody growth. Twig and sprout are synonyms.

SLIP   See Cutting.

SPUR   The stubby twig-like wood on which the fruit is borne on certain species of fruit trees. Examples of such trees are apples, pears, plums, and apricots.

SPUR-TYPE   A sub-variety of a fruit, often apple, characterized by having more than the usual number of spurs, some of them frequently occurring on the trunk as well as on the limbs.

STAMEN   That part of a flower that bears the pollen; thus the male part. See Pollination.

STANDARD   A regular-sized fruit tree. Not dwarf size.

STEMPIECE   A piece of living wood grafted to another tree to form a part or all of that tree's trunk. The most common reasons for doing this are to dwarf a tree, by using a stempiece taken from a natural dwarf; or to provide a compatible link between the rootstock and the scion that becomes the top of the tree.

STOCK   The part of a tree to which a scion is grafted. Because this part usually includes the roots, "rootstock" is the term most commonly used.

SUCKER   A shoot arising from a root; this shoot is usually pruned off and discarded.

TERMINAL   The farthest-out and consequently newest growth on a branch or trunk.

THINNING   A removal of unwanted fruit or branches from a tree. The purpose of thinning fruit is to get better size and quality from the remaining fruits. When branches are thinned, it is usually to eliminate crowding or to let sunlight into the tree.

TREE   Technically, a woody plant in which a single trunk is surmounted by a many-branched top.

WATERSPROUT   A fairly vertical and fast-growing limb in the interior of a treetop. Although the appearance of a watersprout is an indication of tree vigor, it is commonly pruned off because it keeps some sunlight out of the tree, and too-vertical limbs are not likely to bear fruit.

WHIP   A young tree, ready for transplanting, consisting of a single, unbranched stem.

INDEX